Robert J. Moore
Award-Winning, Best Selling Author

Magnetic Entrepreneur

Mastermind

MAGNETIC ENTREPRENEUR

Robert J. Moore
Award-Winning, Best Selling Author

Magnetic Entrepreneur

Mastermind

Legal Disclaimer

Copyright © 2019 Robert J. Moore. All rights reserved worldwide.

No part of this material may be used, reproduced, distributed or transmitted in any form and by any means whatsoever, including without limitation photocopying, recording or other electronic or mechanical methods or by any information storage and retrieval system, without the prior written permission from the author, except for brief excerpts in a review. This book is intended to provide general information only. Neither the author nor publisher provides any legal or other professional advice. If you need professional advice, you should seek advice from the appropriate licensed professional. This book does not provide complete information on the subject matter covered. This book is not intended to address specific requirements, either for an individual or an organization. This book is intended to be used only as a general guide, and not as a sole source of information on the subject matter. While the author has undertaken diligent efforts to ensure accuracy, there is no guarantee of accuracy or of no errors, omissions or typographical errors. Any slights of people or organizations are unintentional. The author and publisher shall have no liability or responsibility to any person or entity and hereby disclaim all liability, including without limitation, liability for consequential damages regarding any claim, loss or damage that may be incurred, or alleged to have been incurred, directly or indirectly, arising out of the information provided in this book.

Connect with Robert J. Moore
https://www.facebook.com/magneticentrepreneur
www.linkedin.com/in/magneticentrepreneur
E-Mail: info@magneticentrepreneurinc.com

Copyright © 2019 by Robert J. Moore
All rights reserved. No part of this publication may be reproduced or transmitted in any form or by any means, electronic, or mechanical, including photocopying, recording, or by any information storage and retrieval system.

MASTERMIND

This book is dedicated to all the courageous
entrepreneurs who take risks and are willing
to face all obstacles and overcome them.
You are the true magnetic ones.

Acknowledgements

First of all, I would like to thank amazing leaders like Les Brown, Raymond Aaron, Bob Proctor, Eric Thomas, Ted McGrath, Mel Robbins, The Ziglar Family, and Kyle Wilson and many more. Not only are they true Magnetic Entrepreneurs, but they freely share their knowledge with others. Without these mentors in my life, I wouldn't be where I am today.

This book series would not be possible without the great contributions of the co-authors. They are real-life examples of people who started out sometimes with nothing and now are not only successful businesspeople but also experts in their own right.

Thank you for letting your entrepreneurial spirit shine through and encouraging others by sharing your stories and lessons learned. You are an inspiration to all who will read this book!

To Todd Stottlemyre: You are an inspiration to us all. Your ground-breaking work is seen all over the world, and your expertise overall really benefits us all. Thank you for contributing your foreword to this book.

Finally, to you, the reader: No book comes alive until it is read. Thank you for investing in yourself and your future. You will never regret that.

Robert J. Moore
Founder of Magnetic Entrepreneur Inc.™

Table of Contents

Table of Contents

Acknowledgements vii
Table of Contents ix
Foreword xi
    Todd Stottlemyre
Introduction xiii
From Rock Bottom to Sharing World-Class Stages with Top Achievers 1
    Robert J. Moore 6
My Journey from Deep Darkness to Marvelous Light 7
    Alan Wade 15
The Conflict of the Minds 17
    Ronda Lauer 28
Falling Through the Cracks 31
    Alan Brogreen 41
Overcoming Shame 43
    B.W. Lamey 52
The Lead™ Technique 53
    Sameh Hassan 58
Breaking Free from the Captivity of Limited Thinking 61
    Charlene Lovegrove 72
Rize Up 75
    Corey Phair 84

Spirit of a Wounded Child 85
   Preeti Chopra..96
The Celebrity Coach 97
   Pravin Patel..102
The Weekend That Changed my Life 105
   Stephine Ricker 115
Conclusion 116

Foreword

As a former professional athlete, I have found that entrepreneurship and professional sports are very similar when it comes to creating success. Learning to fail your way to success is essential. There will be many ups and downs along the way. The key is to learn from each failure because the failures represent your greatest teacher. Failures are the refinery process that is necessary to become the champion in your field. Each failure represents a new lesson to what you need to get better at in order to achieve your greatest results.

My father, Mel Stottlemyre, a 5x all-star and 5x world champion in Major League baseball taught me many years ago that success boils down to mastering a handful of things. I call these daily behaviours. The key for you is to figure out what those behaviours are in your field and work them every day. One of the best ways is to not only learn from your experience but the experience and expertise of others who have created the success that you are striving for.

Robert J. Moore has co-authored this book in order to guide you in your journey towards your world champion success. Magnetic Entrepreneur is brilliantly structured with fifteen different entrepreneurs who not only took risks but overcame the obstacles to defeat the odds. I would highly suggest studying these stories and learn how each entrepreneur used their lessons and the great challenges they had to overcome to propel them to their purpose in life. Each chapter will inspire and impact your life as long as you have an open mind and are willing to put one foot in front of another.

It is my life purpose to serve, inspire, and impact others in helping them live out all of their dreams and live their championship lives. The key is not in how many times you fall down but in how many times you get back up so don't ever quit on yourself. Be RELENTLESS.

Todd Stottlemyre
Former MLB player
3x World Champion
Author of Bestselling book *Relentless Success*
Speaker
Entrepreneur
Https://toddofficial.com/erica
www.facebook.com/todd.stottlemyre
Instagram todd.stott

Introduction

Finding good partners is the key to success in anything: in business, in marriage and, especially, in investing.

– Robert Kiyosaki

Business has dramatically changed in the last twenty years. It is a whole new world out there where there is the opportunity for anyone to grow an amazing business that creates financial freedom. No longer is it only big businesses that make all the money. With the advent of the internet, a whole new environment has been created where anyone with the right skills and training can become successful.

That is where the magnetic entrepreneur comes in. Old-school business techniques no longer work, and just throwing money into television and print ads do not bring the results wanted.

Why?

People are hungry for more. They are tired of being treated like brainless, second-class citizens who mindlessly follow whatever advertising tells them to do. The internet has now given them endless choices on how and where they spend their money. They can do research and make decisions on companies without ever entering their doors. One bad review, from the right person, on the wrong site and their sales can drop dramatically.

Customers and clients are tired of the crap. They want to work with and buy from entrepreneurs and companies that they know, like, and trust. They want to be treated as if they matter. This is why being a magnetic entrepreneur is essential for success in today's world.

You Must Be More

What does it mean to be "magnetic"?

In the Merriam-Webster dictionary (www.merriam-webster.com/dictionary), it says:

Possessing an extraordinary power or ability to attract.

Some people naturally have a magnetic personality that does help in business but, if you look at the wording, it also says "ability". That means that there is hope. It is not only naturally-gifted people who can succeed; anyone who wants to learn how, can.

But …

You must be willing to become more. That is where most people get stuck. They want to stay the way that they are and reap the rewards of the wealthy. There is a reason why, so few people attain it. There is a cost to be a successful entrepreneur: you must become someone you are not.

There are things that you are going to have to let go of, and there are things that you are going to have to master through practice. There is no easy road to prosperity. You must earn it.

What sort of things are you going to have to let go of?

➢ Fear in all forms
➢ Poverty Mindset
➢ Not Enough Mindset
➢ Laziness
➢ Perfectionism
➢ Self-Doubt

These are only a few to get you started. Two hindrances will hold you back from success: what goes on in your head and heart, and the skills and actions you need to get to where you want to go. When you conquer these, success can't help but come to you.

What will you have to master?

Communication Skills

One thing that differentiates successful entrepreneurs from others is their ability to communicate effectively with everyone. They speak carefully and consider their words before they come out of their mouth.

Emotional Control

Things will go wrong in business. The one who overcomes is the one who can control their heart. They don't overreact or take it personally; they step back, take an honest look at the situation, and then come up with a plan to fix things. Which leads to …

Unending Learning

Profound achievers get that way because every roadblock is an opportunity to learn and become more. They recognize that there is a solution to every problem; they just have to figure out what it is.

Sales Skills

You can be an entrepreneur and not know how to sell. However, anything that you do, and you don't sell, is a hobby. You do it because you enjoy it, but you don't necessarily make money from it. In order to be financially successful, especially as a solopreneur, you must be able to sell, or you won't have a business at all; just something you are good at.

Relationship Building Skills

You must recognize that your business will be built upon the relationships that you make with prospects, leads, customers, clients and other entrepreneurs. Each one requires a different skill, and you must master them all. Does it seem overwhelming? Don't let it get to you. Becoming a magnetic entrepreneur is a process that happens over time. You don't learn and implement everything in a week.

That is where all the authors in this book come in. They have "been there" and "done that" and are sharing their knowledge with you. They know the shortcuts and pitfalls that we all experience and are sharing their stories so you can succeed faster than they did.

Each author is an expert who has been at the bottom and worked their way up. Each one had to overcome significant obstacles and become more than they ever could imagine. In the pages of this book, you will learn from them what it means to become a truly magnetic entrepreneur.

Are you ready for an incredible journey? Are you ready to be propelled forward? Then turn the page and let's get started.

-Robert J. Moore

From Rock Bottom to Sharing World-Class Stages with Top Achievers

by Robert J. Moore

I was totally destitute. Homeless and alone, I had alienated my friends and family with my delinquent behaviour and had nowhere to turn. I thought my journey was over, and my path was at a dead end.

When I was 12 years old, my dad walked into the room and told me and my brothers that our mom was not our biological mother. As a result, I created a story in my head, thinking it was all clear now, that "my mom did not love me since I was not her child." I began to feel like I was alone, angry, and suddenly, as though I did not fit in. I felt this was the reason why I was always getting yelled at and grounded.

This thought had a deep effect on how I viewed myself. I had low self-esteem for a long period of time. I acted very irresponsibly and did not consider any of the consequences of my actions until it was too late.

I was 17 years old when I first got into a decent romantic relationship. I had an amazing job and was drinking less alcohol. Just after I turned 20, my girlfriend started to go into labour, then went into an epileptic seizure and died in my hands. I realized that being with someone you love at the point of their death is a profound experience.

Nonetheless, I found it to be very emotional and mentally exhausting. During grief counselling, I had learned these feelings are a normal and understandable response to a very stressful situation.

I said to myself, "Wow, what am I going to do with my life?" It seemed that every time I got close to someone; they were taken away. This was when I started to use booze and drugs to suppress my feelings.

After feeling sorry for myself for a number of years, I decided I wanted to become someone, and I moved to a treatment center in a new town to get the help I needed. Once I became clean and sober in 2005, I became overwhelmed with emotions as all of my emotions started to thaw out.

Years later, after a lot of inner and outer work, I did end up accomplishing a number of credentials including becoming a social service worker, achieving an addiction diploma, graduating with a bachelor's and master's degree in psychology, earning my Neuro-Linguistic Programming (NLP) Master Practitioner Certification, and receiving an honorary doctorate degree.

These milestones played a big part in changing my behaviour and my negative outlook. This took me back to when I was 12 years old and my dad told me mom was not my biological mother.

My experience of this was that my parents did not love me and wanted to punish me for something, but I realize now that, in fact, they did love me, as they were the ones raising me and my two brothers. They put food on the table and clothing on our backs and would try to help with our homework.

I did not need to take drugs or alcohol to clearly see the truth, as this moment of realization was very strong. I teared up like Niagara Falls, allowing me to miraculously receive the sense of comfort I had been missing and feel like a huge weight was lifted from my body.

That was my breakthrough. That was the moment it came to me. I then knew that I want to help people. I want to make a difference in the world. I want to coach people. I want to speak on stages to share my message. I truly want to inspire more people to transform their lives and make a massive difference in the world. That's when I realized I would have to start working on myself and start standing for who I am.

I started to study the top influencers in the world to learn how they became successful and what I needed to do to reach their level. Over the last decade, I have studied 46 very successful top influencers and motivational speakers in the world who allowed me to either interview them personally or share the stage with them. What an honour it has been.

One of the top influencers stated in a video, "If I want to be the best, I will have to learn from the best." So, I decided to hire a few of the top life and business coaches. These included the operations manager from *Think and Grow Rich*, Eric Thomas, Ted McGrath, and even Les Brown himself. I ended up getting the first book in my *The Magnetic Entrepreneur* series endorsed by Les Brown and the second book endorsed by Don Green, CEO of Napoleon Hill Foundation.

Chapter two of *Think and Grow Rich* had a significant impact on my life, as it taught me the power of visualization and allowed me to see the end result in my mind.

I dreamt I would meet Les Brown, number one motivational speaker in the world, Bob Proctor, number one for wealth in the world, Douglas Vermeeren, who developed the top three personal development movies in the world, and Raymond Aaron, New York Times bestseller. Not only have I met them, but I have also shared the stage with them. My vision has come true.

All through my life, I wanted to become someone but had no clue where to start. When I started my process of sobriety in 2005, I was told that I had to find my WHY.

By "WHY," I mean, What's your purpose? What's your cause? What's your belief? Why does your organization exist? Why do you get out of bed in the morning? And why should anyone care?

Through school, I had to do many presentations in front of my peers.

Each time I knew I was going to be in front of the class to present, I would feel knots in my stomach. My thoughts would be racing. I would create a PowerPoint slide on the topic. This would help keep the focus off me and allow me to focus on the topic. Surprisingly enough, once I started to present, my nerves seemed to calm down, and I became relaxed enough to finish my presentation.

Today, I am on world-class stages with the top influencers in the world, and it does not make me nervous, as I have learned that the message is not for me. I already know what I am going to say. The message is for the audience.

Today, I am the founder and CEO of Magnetic Entrepreneur Inc™ where I have a number of programs—a magazine, entrepreneur co-authoring program, business mastermind, and red carpet gala event for all Magnetic Entrepreneur authors to gather for an amazing time of knowledge with top speakers from around the globe and to win an award for their hard work.

Studying 46 top achievers, I learned that the old-school business techniques no longer work. When I first began coaching and speaking, I was just throwing money into television and print ads that did not bring the results entrepreneurs want.

We have built mind-blowing programs that have become internationally talked about and have had a lot of well-known celebrities, like CEO of Napoleon Hill Foundation Don Green, former MLB player and 3x World Champion Todd Stottlemyre, New York Times bestselling author Raymond Aaron, and founder of Jim Rohn International Kyle Wilson just to name a few, writing forewords for the *Magnetic Entrepreneur* book series or asking me to join them on world-class stages.

As early-stage entrepreneurs strive for progress, the incredible programs and strategies that Magnetic Entrepreneur Inc™ offers enhance their knowledge and up-brand anyone willing to take on the challenge. I will never forget the challenges I had to take on to become successful, nor will I forget the feeling of being 12 years old and my dad telling me and my brothers that our mom was not our biological mother.

Magnetic Entrepreneur Inc.™ is by far one of the greatest works I have ever created. I am honoured to share it!

Robert J. Moore

Robert J. Moore is the founder of Magnetic Entrepreneur Inc.™ an internationally awarded speaker, and bestselling author. He is an international speaker and business coach that has impacted the lives of over 120,000 people through the work associated with Magnetic Entrepreneur Inc.™ Robert has studied 46 of the top achievers in the world in the past decade to be able to build amazing programs. He states, "My programs are by far one of the greatest works I have ever created. I am honoured to share them with you."

Email - info@magneticentrepreneurinc.com
Linkedin - www.linkedin.com/in/magneticentrepreneur
Facebook - Magnetic Entrepreneur Inc.

My Journey from Deep Darkness to Marvelous Light
by Alan Wade

So many times, I have asked myself, "Wow. How did this happen?" I went from being traumatized as a 10-year-old boy who was raped in church, to someone who lives in complete abundance and peace. I wish I could tell you that it was a comfortable journey, but it wasn't.

I spent the next 17 years living in hell. Regularly, I experienced night terrors, night sweats and living in a total state of fear. The guilt and shame I felt affected every part of my life. When it happened, I didn't understand because I was an innocent 10-year-old, but when I finally comprehended that I was violated, that guilt and shame turned to anger and rage. Over time it became uncontrollable. I also experienced the other side of the coin, where I hated myself and became suicidal. Thankfully, none of my attempts succeeded.

Fast forward to today, I now live a life of abundance and feel a sense of inner peace and happiness. My relationship with my partner in life and business is incredible, and I am a father of six grown children and two grandchildren. I get to vacation and explore the world with those I love a few times a year.

It was an honour to co-author an award-winning book with my partner called *The Magic Within*. We now speak at events and share our vision of hope and offer strategies for people to improve their lives. Our coaching/consulting company brings in over six figures, and the best part of all is that I get paid for doing what I love.

If I wasn't the one living this story, I might not think it is real.

One of the turning points in my life came one day when I was spending time with one of my best friends. He told me that when I became angry, I frightened him. I realized then that something had to change, that I had to change. I did some soul searching and made some changes in my life. The first step on my journey of growth was the realization that I had to change my thinking. This concept was validated when I went to school to study social service work and reaffirmed when I worked as an addiction counsellor.

As time went on, I began to change who I spent time with and what I did with my time. It was during that time that I met my partner. Cindy and I both worked as counsellors in the addiction field, so we had a commonality; however, Cindy also introduced me to spirituality, and she spoke of many different things that intrigued me. She talked about energy and the law of attraction. I wanted to learn more, so I delved into a whole new life of Reiki and the power of vibration. This new way of thinking and living changed my life in new and rewarding ways, and my thinking had become completely radical and magical.

When you become aware of how powerful your thoughts are in creating your life, you will be much more selective in what you think. Your mind is a potent tool, and it can create great joy in your life or great misery. Learning to manage your thoughts is a potent tool. With our coaching program, we spend a lot of time working with an individual's thought systems.

To change my thinking, I had to get honest with myself. I was now no more blaming the world or others for what was going on in my life. I also had to figure out what it was I wanted and what I was willing to do to get it. Part of that process was looking into why I did not feel worthy of abundance. It came down to the fact that it was my internal programming that was stopping me. Forty years ago, I allowed the after-effects from that traumatic event to rule my life for 17 years. It became part of my programming.

Programming comes from your parents, family, friends, teachers, life experiences and the environment you live in. It is a learned behaviour. Most of my programming held me from having the life I wanted. Once you can recognize that your beliefs (programming) are hurting you or keeping you from succeeding, then you can change that mindset. You cannot fix something unless you know what it is that is broken.

To change my thinking about life when I was 27, I had to stop blaming that person for ruining my life. I had to take ownership of everything I had done to that point in my life and let go of the anger. I used positive affirmation to change my life. I paid attention to my thinking daily. When I would have unhealthy thoughts, I would adjust them to positive thoughts. I know this sounds very hard, but it was much easier than you think. I wanted to change so badly that I was willing to do whatever it took.

One of the most powerful affirmations that I used myself, and I now share with my clients is, "I am worthy." I believe that this was one of the most important things I learned to do and one of the main reasons I now live a life of abundance.

After I started saying this affirmation to myself regularly, I realized how deeply I felt that I was not worthy of good things. Upon exploration of this, I realized that this was a deeply ingrained belief that I had been given to as a child. It was my programming!

We are all programmed right from the day we are born; however, most of our beliefs are not our own; they are someone else's. These beliefs can come from your parents, siblings, friends, and teachers, anyone in your life.

My beautifully paved road to abundance manifested when I attended Neuro-Linguistic Programming (NLP) training. That's when it became clear that my old programming was holding me back from creating a life of abundance. There was a part of me that was holding on to someone else's beliefs. My old programming was, "I am not worthy of a life of abundance." It also included getting a job, working hard, very hard if you want a good life, and that money is hard to come by.

Taking that NLP training was one of the best things I did. Becoming a certified NLP practitioner and utilizing the concepts and tools, allowed me to clear my old programming out, and install the, "I am worthy programming." I now use these techniques with my coaching clients to assist in their growth and success.

Writing our award-winning book was also a catalyst for positive change in our life. Doors began to open to many new possibilities. We networked with other like-minded people who were successful in their life. It became apparent to me that the people around me who influenced my life were significant to my success. I learned from these people and found mentors who propelled me to a whole new level of awareness.

The law of attraction teaches that like attracts like. I was attracting likeminded people into my life, wealthy, successful, spiritual people. I took advantage of training that would benefit my growth and success. The more that I learned, the more I was able to apply the law of attraction in my life. The energy work that I had absorbed and utilized was working. My positive outlook and expectations of a beautiful life were manifesting before my eyes!

I remember meeting our first real client. After our initial interview and deciding to work with him, I had to determine how much my time was worth. I remember calling his father, who had made the referral. I recall him asking me what my rate was. I know this is going to sound strange, but it seemed like minutes went by as I was thinking how much I was worth.

I remember feeling panicked a bit. You know that feeling of your face becoming red when you're put on the spot, well, I experienced that as well. Then suddenly, I remembered my mentor saying that I could make ten times what I make an hour. The next thing I blurted out what my rate would be, and he did not even flinch, he accepted it and said, "Thank you that's great." I remember getting off the phone and asking myself, "Did that just happen?"

Working as an addiction and mental health worker, your hourly rate is not going to make you rich or create abundance. Most people have heard the phrase, JOB, just over broke. That was what I was. It was my change in thinking that created this new abundance in my life, and this is the great secret. It is the first thing you have to do.

Abundance does come to you when you start thinking and feeling abundant. If you do not feel abundant, then abundance will not come to you. That is why I pointed out that I expected success to come to me. I could feel a change in my vibration, and I was in resonance with my desires.

After I was able to change my thinking to I am worthy and feeling worthy, abundance began to manifest in our life. I remember telling the next client we got how much we charge, and it seemed to flow out just like water with no hesitation. This income became my normal way of living.

My journey to this lifestyle has been very gratifying and to say the least interesting. I realize today the power of the unconscious mind and how it works in our life. NLP works with the unconscious mind to create change. Words are also compelling in the process of creation. When I was at the NLP training, I decided to change my passwords (commonly used, positive or negative phrases that we don't even think about). I used to use the password "shit happens." I decided to change my passwords to "abundance," and almost immediately, my financial situation changed!

The thing that sticks in my mind is that I made decisions. I decided that I didn't want to frighten people anymore. I made the decision that I wanted to have a healthy relationship with a wonderful and compatible partner. I decided that I wanted to grow, heal and learn, and I began my journey into the psychological and spiritual world. I decided that I wanted more, that I deserved more, and the opportunity to write a book landed in my lap.

The key is when you decide to do something different and the opportunity knocks, you have to take action. Yes, I was petrified to write a book and talk about the most devastating thing that happened to me. I felt like I was stripped naked and baring my soul to the world. But that is what we have to do to heal our wounds and become more. I encourage my clients to share their deepest darkest secrets with me, so they can move past their fear and pain and become the amazing person that is waiting inside of them. To present to the world who they truly are.

We all are truly amazing and beautiful. We all have magic within. You have to tap into your true inner you. I did, and my life is amazingly full of all of the beautiful things that I can imagine. Yes, I imagined all of this, our imagination is the creator of our life, so imagine greatness!

Use your all-powerful mind to believe the best life possible for you. BE the extraordinary person that you were born to BE.

If I can do it, you can. I was a boy who was traumatized at an early age. I was lost in a world of fear and pain. I found that little boy and I loved him, told him he is worthy of a great life. Yes, I have financial abundance, and I have an abundant life of love, happiness, family, health and spirituality. I know that you can do this too. It is within you, and the magic is within you.

Alan Wade

Alan is a professional Speaker, Coach, and the co-author of the award-winning book, *The Magic Within - How to Transform Your Life*. Alan has also co-authored another book with International Bestselling author, Robert J. Moore. *Awakening – Out of the Darkness into the Light*.

Alan has years of experience working in the addictions and mental health field. He shares his knowledge and wisdom at speaking engagements. He is known to use humour and common sense to connect with his audience and inspire change. His primary goal is to help others in overcoming their fears and motivating them to take the first steps towards transforming their own lives.

In his books, Alan reveals his traumatic childhood experience of sexual abuse. He talks about this painful event and how he has overcome his past to the point that it does not negatively impact his life today.

Alan specializes in First Nation culture, he is a certified practitioner of Neuro-Linguistic Programming (NLP), he is Reiki Master, and studies various other spiritual practices. He uses his education, real-life experience, and spiritual teachings to help others.

Alan is a loving father and family man. He loves to travel. He especially enjoys riding his motorcycle and the adventure and freedom that comes with it.

The Conflict of the Minds
by Ronda Lauer

The mind, a queer sort of house, the host of our conscious and subconscious minds. ~Ronda Lauer

She has learned many lessons over the decades of her life. A child of great curiosity and joy, she put a smile on many onlookers as they would observe her at play, frolicking in the long grass in the apple orchard; taking her long walks in the beautifully scented evergreen bush where it smelled like Christmas all year long; where the chickadees sang to her the same yet unusual song, "chick-a-dee-dee-dee." She felt connected to her surroundings, where there were peace and solitude, where she heard no more, the banters of her family. She loved the texture of the blanketing of pine needles underfoot, as she would step ever so softly in the hopes of having the curious chickadees land on her hands, and perhaps to see a deer or two grazing in the cornfield just beyond the magical trail.

The squirrels were always silly and playful, and the occasional hawk would be seen flying overhead. There were many chickens and rodents to help sustain the birds of prey. Her father would occasionally take his rifle "outback" to see if he could shoot down his trophy, the menacing feathered beast who would attempt to pierce his chickens, with its long, sharp talons. He took great pride in raising the fowl with white plumage to feed his family throughout the winter months. He did this with love, without ill-intent of causing harm. She appreciated how much he loved the hobby farm, and the fur and feather babies.

Sadly, he also raised many snow-white rabbits, and she remembers them growing so large. Again, he would take great care in his beasts, although her heart, would often break. She, as a young girl, would participate in the slaughter, to help the family and obey her father. It was a way of life, but one that she would eventually choose to do without. She fell in love with every goat, dog, pigeon, chicken, duck, pig and calf, and oh the rabbits!!! Her love of the calm and peace of the bunnies she knew, she would carry into many years to come. The cats, she more or less tolerated, she loved them too, but bonded differently with their independent nature, nonetheless.

She recalls a tiny baby chick, one that was deformed at birth with its crooked little feet, hobbling and falling over as it would walk. She felt so horrid for it that it did not have the same sort of chance at life, as short as that may be for a meat chicken. She made a decision that has tugged at her heart all of her life. She decided at the time that the chopping block and the axe (which was sharpened by an old fashioned grinding rock wheel) would help to put the sweet little creature out of its misery, as the others always pecked at it and caused it such considerable pain and anguish. It was bullied as occurs in nature, to eliminate the weak. It was just a matter of time that its life would be over; she just helped to speed up the process out of compassion. She buried the fragile little chick at the back of the family property and didn't dare ever tell a soul. Her heart collapsed at what she had done. That which she had been taught, year after year after year, was ingrained in her subconscious mind, and without a thought, the deed was done.

Her compassion for anything with a beating heart was awakened that day. There lay an unexplainable discomfort, a feeling of embarrassment, and something that just felt inauthentic with her own beating heart. She exuded love everywhere she went, although this was a completely different experience for her. She made friends with everyone but paid particular attention to those who were not the "popular" group amongst the clicks. She observed the same sort of bullying in the form of exclusion, silent treatments and the occasional brawl when one individual felt that their power was beyond the level of others. She felt the injustice in the proverbial "pecking order" that the human race was capable of, and she did not share the same viewpoint at all. She befriended those who were most unlikely to have friends because she felt strongly that they were all one, and that everyone deserves that same feeling of love, inclusion and safety.

As she grew into her teenage years, having listened to the growing altercations within the household, a determination to stand up for what was right hit home, although it wasn't until well after a young man in the family sexually abused her. She did not stand up for her rights then, and struggled most of her adult years to do so, out of fear, although there was an emerging inner conflict, possibly apparent to others, and then again, perhaps not. She did not quite grasp the conundrum. Truth be told, she found it easier to stand up for the rights of others, to be the friend that no one else could muster because they were different or didn't seem to fit in for whatever reason. She was a soft place to land for others, yet she didn't quite know how to love herself, and therefore put everyone else first. There was something that was ingrained in her subconscious, that she wasn't worthy, because of this young man's acts against her, and a plethora of other impactful occurrences that had contributed in her young years. The mind-frick rogue had been created.

She recalls in her early teen years that a flu bug had affected her, as is a normal occurrence in anyone's life. As usual, as it was, an unusual recurrence was manifested day after day. She had created a cycle of being violently ill, a pattern that SHE had created. Every day for weeks, she would be sick at the same time of the day, observing the hour on the clock, or the same television show being on when she had been previously ill, and the power that took over her mind would chant: "it was just yesterday at this time that I had been sick." The mere thought of it kept her in the bondage of sorts, and she would again repeat the motions of running to the nearest bathroom to be violently ill. It was repulsive, and not understood by anyone else but her. This went on for far too long. It got so bad that the family doctor was called on one of the worst evenings, and she did a house call, a procedure that is not likely these days. When the older female doctor arrived at the rural household, she gave the weary girl a medication, with her mother standing with concern in the background of the chilled basement bathroom, in needle form to help ease the wretched discomfort — getting needles from that point on created a certain degree of anxiety for her. An obnoxious procedure, yet somehow it helped. She didn't want to repeat this torturous act any longer. She can easily recall having to work on what was going on in her mind, a repeat story of when she was sick last, to watching the clock, to being sick again ... she realized that it was almost a form of personal sabotage.

This young lady, intuitively realized through the pain and trauma of her adolescent years, that by being mindful of her thoughts, that she was able to alter the outcome of what had become a repeat pattern for quite some time. This had nothing to do with a poor body image, but what she believes to have been trapped emotions that were dying to get out. When the image and timing of the day before she entered her mind, she practiced deep breathing and would attempt to distract where her mind was taking her. It was truly miraculous, as these practices were not taught, nor talked about in those days. Eventually, the story became less and less impactful on her psychological self, and she was able to curb the urges, day after day, week after week, month after month, although, to date, she can't be near those particular sounds of someone being ill for obvious reasons, to her.

As surprising as it was, the outcome was that of self-healing. It isn't that she had recognized what was going on consciously or subconsciously, as she was still just a girl. There was a time where she recalls being so angry and frustrated, at God knows what now, she cannot recall, but what she does remember is running to the downstairs basement and hiding behind a sofa. It was there that she took her fingernails of both hands and scraped them down both sides of her tender face. She had red lines running down her cheeks for days. It was intriguing to her that her emotional pain was but for a moment, the lesser of the two evils. This is NOT a recommendation put forth AT ALL. It is unfortunate looking back at her story, seeing the pain and trauma, and her feeling like it wasn't safe to share. She bottled up her anguish for decades; her mini upsets, the negativity of some who were close to her, and the massive trauma that today would be dealt with immediately by professionals. Her childlike joy was taken advantage of and she was seen as a weak and innocent youngster, an easy target.

It took many years of her stuffing her pain into the gloomy and heavy backpack that she carried in her soul. No one ever understood, for a good reason. People don't know what they don't know. Her confidence would gradually improve, to be knocked down again by those that she seemed to love the most. She lived through a great deal of negative onlookers who were jealous of her good-natured and kind loving ways, again an easy target for naysayers and narcissists. She was a unique little gal, who wound up being the punching bag of sorts for those who chose to be deceitful and manipulative toward her. They seemed to have known that with her low level of confidence, she lacked assertiveness. She was not of an aggressive nature that's for sure!! She was more the type that would wave off the hurtful implications, not addressing her true feelings, and carry on. The unfortunate side effect of such a coping mechanism is that the soul eventually gets tired and the body and the mind begin to reflect that inner pain. It is like a self-perpetuating prophecy, suppress, stuff and eventually get sick, or at the least, sick and tired.

What she eventually came to realize, and this was through an assertiveness training course a decade into her adult years after she went through burnout and the collapse that woke her up, that it was time to stop; it was time to say "no" to that which she didn't agree with or that did not resonate with her. After she hit the floor of her bathroom and suffered a concussion; as a result, she learned that standing her ground really did not make her mean or selfish, but rather that it was her own unique right. Every single person on this planet has the same right. What was learned during this training was that it wasn't necessarily about her confidence either, but that she may have lacked self-respect, and self-love. It all makes sense to her now, but it was like unravelling a tangled ball of kite string. Intriguing as it was, she took the human out of the person, again but for a time. She gave compliments quickly, yet struggled in receiving them. She gave of herself, to her detriment in time and energy. She would allow the critics to steal her power, yet she would not be able to share criticism, even if constructive. It was also interesting that she'd apologize for situations that had nothing to do with her ... as she attempted to soften the opportunity for a positive outcome, whilst justifying her tender behaviour to others.

She had been used to some pretty heavy authoritative demands when young, whereby loud, threatening and harsh tones kept her in a state of fear. It most certainly wasn't all of the time, yet when times were challenging, this was what she had to face. She recalls fists banging on tabletops and a hole being put in her bedroom door when she barricaded herself in her room for self-protection. Perhaps at age 13 or 14, she recalls enormous anger toward her by a family member that she thought someone was going to get injured badly by the throwing of a huge log that was initially meant for a stoked fire in the fireplace. No wonder fear was a state that was repeated throughout her young years and into adulthood. She never wanted to "rock the boat" for fear of being misunderstood or worse yet, threatened. Attempts at rational conversation even as a young married woman would lead to the silent treatment by her "then" husband, another form of aggression, believe it or not.

She is so grateful that through her life journey to date, that she has become more assertive. She recognizes that she has rights, as does anyone else, and that she too matters!! She allows herself to have a judgement, without judging others per se. She recognizes that she has the right to be respected and that she, too, may share her personal feelings without being chastised for such. She has come to the realization that she may respond with a "yes" or a "no" based on her feelings and that she need not feel guilty!! She has the right!! She recognizes that she deserves to be heard and taken seriously. She sees clearly that she may change her mind on a matter, and that she need not provide a reason as to the justification. Here is a biggy, that she now sees that she too is allowed to err and be responsible for her own mistakes. She understands now, that she may choose not to answer specific questions, that she may be independent, and that she can take a break and create an environment of self-love and compassion for herself ... to be pampered!! She has every single right!!!!

Do you realize that it is YOUR right, to create an environment of joy and happiness in your own life and that you too, may break free from the mental anguish that has held you back? You may, at any given time, choose to live with more self-compassion, to raise the bar and live a life where you truly love and honour yourself, and that you respect YOU for all of your talents AND flaws, and others will follow suit and share that same sentiment!! Why would others choose to give to you that which you do not deliver to yourself? This is a very arguable statement, almost as in which came first, the chicken or the egg, the horse or the cart. It is an encompassing form of infinity ... there is no known starting point and no endpoint, but it continues until the cycle is broken.

Since her time of self-discovery, she has realized that by meditating and including mindfulness in her daily routine, as well as through implementing prayer into her life, that she has created a calm and cleansed soul, needless to say, a refreshed state of mind. It wasn't easy for her, as the prior conditioning would creep in to play havoc if she were to remain unaware. That awareness has become a key ingredient to her overall health and success in life. It is because of the patience of learning self-love and respect alike, that her soul now feels more like the purity of a freshly fallen blanket of snow. No longer is vulnerability a bad term, as a matter of fact, it is embraced. It is through her choice of being vulnerable that she is shining her beautiful light, and being the most authentic woman that she has ever been in her lifetime.

Self-care is not a selfish act and is mandatory for our survival. Her awareness in this area has also been instrumental in her healing. She chooses to go for walks in nature and go back to listening to the chickadees on a path in a bush where the ground is soft to walk on, where the sun peers through the rustling of the leaves on the trees. She delights in loving on all of the animals, in creating the connection of pure love. She has re-engaged in playing her music and singing to her heart's content, despite her imperfections, for perfectionism no longer holds her captive. She sleeps as her body requires, and is not forced to awake before she is ready. She has engaged in her fitness regime, which increases not only her level of circulation but dopamine and endorphins, those happy hormones that help to create and stimulate her "happy place." She has lost her unwanted weight and has chosen a healthy plant-based diet. She has chosen the stance that positive relationships are all that she desires to be surrounded by, whether family or friends or in her field of work.

Although an accumulation of pain and trauma may have occurred, what most people don't realize is that we all have the opportunity to rewire our brain. You can train your mind, slay those dragons that were holding you captive by recognizing your thoughts, realizing what changes may need to occur, and make the necessary changes!!! It is said that we only use approximately 5% of our conscious mind in our daily life. That means that 95% is what is dictating how we do and deal with our everyday choices and thoughts. You are the change you wish for. BE the change for pity's sake ... before you allow your life to waste away with limiting beliefs. You ARE unlimited potential. Learn and grow. Train hard and become the best version of you possible. Break free ... it is your time ... your life ... your choice, and then teach our children the same principles for an abundant life.

Ronda Lauer

Ronda Lauer is a successful transformational coach, Certified through the Certified Coaches Federation, who appeals to those who have been stuck in life. She has wrestled with adversity in her past and has been a resilient warrior in conquering her many battles and life lessons. She has been in several near-death experiences yet is living her purpose. You may wish to visit your relationships, improve on your parenthood skills, re-establish healthy boundaries, cover your finances, consider a career change, improve on your fitness and health or discover some amazing new habits. Perhaps it is deeper, and you wish to move beyond your current limiting beliefs!!

Ronda is a life coach extraordinaire, who brings her talent and compassion into her coaching sessions in order to see the goals and dreams you have, come to fruition. Care to eliminate your stinking thinking and move to greater heights? You make the move and connect with her if you are open to moving beyond that which you have always known and explore the world of opportunity and possibilities!! Be hungry ... be the change you wish to see…

She is a Platinum member of the Healthy Wealthy and Wise Coaching Program and is in the Million Dollar Coaching Program through the Healthy Wealthy and Wise Corporation. Want to learn more? Today is your day so make every moment count!!!!

There is so much beauty and there are so many amazing things in this world. She never stops exploring, experiencing and learning.

She strives to take the best care of herself, her kids and her environment.

She began writing a book about the experiences of her husband's illness. She is amazed at how much she enjoys writing and is very excited to share her story with the world. So, keep an eye out for her book hitting the shelf!

You are never alone with a coach like Ronda by your side.

Ronda Lauer

Connect with her via Facebook or LinkedIn, or even better:
www.rideofyourlife.today
rondalauer@gmail.com

Falling Through the Cracks
by Alan Brogreen

It was the summer of 2014, and just two months prior, Ronda and I were at the oncologist office in London, Ontario, where I was given an all-clear bill of health! No more Cancer! We were so elated we both wept tears of joy! Now back to the summer, I was returning home from my work as an automotive and aerospace engineer when my phone rang. I pulled over to the shoulder to take the call, and to my surprise, it was my oncologist! In the space of a millisecond, I went through every possible scenario, she spoke softly "and, Al, we did not get it all," and I received yet another date with the surgeon. I completely fell apart; we had only received the news two weeks prior, enjoy your life, live to a hundred! It took me over a half-hour to regain my composure; I called my wife and explained as gently as I could our new circumstances. My partner left her work immediately and met me at home.

You see, I have been through a ton of adversity in my life and on March 05 of 1998, my first spiritual awakening. I was to find recovery from the despair of alcoholism, drug addiction, illegal prescription medications, a false belief of who I was and the addiction to MORE! So here I am, on a hot summer afternoon with a magnum of wine, as of yet unopened. Ronda came home and found me shaken to the core with the bottle of unopened wine, I asked her if she would join me, and she replied no! She pleaded for me not to open the bottle until she called our daughter, an addictions counsellor, and I half-heartedly and regretfully agreed.

Brittany was to show up with our daughter-in-law, and they enlightened me on every reason, not go through with drinking the wine. Everyone was afraid I would never come back! I could not reconcile the cancer news and popped the wine open, poured it into a small glass; I tipped it towards my lips, knowing I was in danger of another kind altogether.

There was weeping and crying, by all of us. I hadn't noticed the three women in my life had retired inside. Ronda joined me a while later and eventually joined me in a glass. You see, Ronda does not have a problem with alcohol. She told me that Brittany and Fiona had left. It affected Fiona terribly as she had been affected by alcohol early in her life, and she couldn't understand what I was going through, and I don't blame her. My stepdaughter, in all her wisdom, asked her mom if there was any more booze in the house. She took Ronda's wine home with her and left knowing that my mind was so full I had nowhere else to go.

I lit a fire and continued to drink slowly, determined to remove myself from what I was feeling: the emotional pain, the angst, the complete and utter uncontrolled misery I found myself in. Talk about the poor ME's. I had every right to feel this way, again scared as hell. Ronda joined me in a glass, and eventually, the bottle lay empty. She asked me if I was OK to go for a walk, and I replied, "Yes." We instead held each other up as we strolled (kind of funny in hindsight). We ended up in the backyard of a couple we respect dearly. Mary and Terry listened intently, shared with us, prayed with us, fed us and made sure we got home safely. I most certainly do not remember what we talked about, only that tomorrow was a new day, and I would not drink again, and that was to hold. Still, the silent hand was at work in all of my affairs. Some would call it God, others alignment with the universe, and others yet a connection to Mother Earth.

My surgeon called the next morning, and I again was scheduled for surgery. I took a month off from a position in a quality management company that serviced medical supplies and the aerospace and automotive sector. When I arrived at my first project a week after surgery, my colleague noticed I was bleeding through my shirt on my left side near my belt line. I had inner and outer stitches, and the internal stitches had let go! I had to excuse myself, go to the nearest hospital and have my incision cared for. All the while, I was beginning to have symptoms of another sort, painful hands, wrists, my shoulders, hips, knees and feet were incredibly sore to the touch. I had localized swelling, body pain, brain fog so thick I could no longer work. I was to fall into a deep depression. Then the pharmaceuticals began, trials of Sulphasazaline, Lyrica, Gabapentin, followed by morphine, Percocet's, Tramadol, Tramacet, Tylenol 3, benzodiazepines, followed by four types of heart and blood pressure pills, 16 prescriptions with no diagnosis! I saw specialist after specialist, and finally, after two years received a diagnosis of fibromyalgia. Fibromyalgia is only diagnosed by testing for other illnesses like arthritis, lupus and Lyme disease, to name a few. From the fall of 2014 until the winter of 2016, I was to remain stuck in my illness, the need to claim personal bankruptcy, a mountain of bills and an uncertain future. All I could think of was my Ronda. I was so sorry and had feelings of guilt over my health. We discussed our future, and we certainly had some stressed conversations. She chose me, and I am ever so grateful and humbled.

Ronda, by this time, had NINE, Yes 9 part-time jobs to try to make ends meet! I went to every place humanly possible to receive help so we wouldn't lose our house. We were refused; I did not qualify for ODSP, Trillium Benefits, or any other support for that matter. We subsequently fell through all the so-called safety nets in our society of living in Ontario. I was to receive top-notch medical and mental health care, and maintain my sobriety from that summer night, spend all of my savings and still, almost lose our house. I didn't qualify for any funding whatsoever because my partner's nine part-time jobs earned over $30,000.00!!! Our future looked as grim as it could. In a short period of time, and I don't have a good recollection of the dates; however, I believe it was the early winter of 2016, and my Ronda was to collapse in the bathroom, smack her body and head violently to the floor, where she received a concussion. Now it was her turn! Paramedics and Fire Men attended Ronda in our living room at three in the morning, and she was transported to the hospital. It was approximately 4 am. I drove to the hospital on all of my medications, it was sleeting, and freezing rain was coming down, the roads were treacherous, I was in no condition to drive because every evening I ended up being filled with sleeping and pain medications. Adrenalin took over, and I drove.

Here we are, of both us off work, and no income! Scared! Heck ya! My partner was to receive health benefits, which helped, and by that time, I had entrusted a lawyer to help me claim CPP Disability Pension. It was to be a redeeming feature as we felt our backs come away from the wall, just a little! Ronda started to recover slowly, and I was still floating between the bed, the couch and our fire pit, even very heavily medicated. Spring of 2017 was to hit me with depression I had never experienced before, and that I ended up having a full out mental health incident, which put me in hospital for three weeks — again another pill for what ails me. I was to attend CBT training, meditation therapy, learn about mindfulness, and connection to nature, along with many appointments with counsellors and several psychiatrists. This medication was so powerful it kept me so out of it, friends and family thought I was using drugs to escape again. I even was called an old stupid stoner. In one regard, 'I was stoned, I hated it, and my hands were tied.'

The next year was to find me in the same place, couch, bed or deck. Ronda enrolled me into a group for senior citizens, and I would do activities and eat with them throughout the week. Ronda then reached out to an old friend, and she joined the Healthy Wealthy and Wise Coaching Program. She instantly found support and a groove that aligned with her morally, physically and spiritually! She was guided and loved back to health by her coach and her new tribe. We adopted through time, a whole food plant-based diet, which she introduced slowly, and by late 2018, we were about 90 to 95% plant-based. Ronda slowly planted seeds with me, "Are you happy?" "Are you OK with your life?" "Is this what you want?" She was always kind and gentle with me, and that assisted yet another miracle to happen!

March of 2019, coincidentally the same month I got clean and sober, 21 years earlier, should probably have been a sign for me! I met with my psychiatrist, and he removed the dreaded 'olanzapine". I had no idea how powerful this anti-psychotic medication was. I ended up in bed in the fetal position, sick for weeks from withdrawal symptoms. These withdrawals were nothing compared to getting off alcohol, cocaine and crack. I was ill for a month, and then, out of now-where *came to some clarity*; I had lost 20 pounds without trying! We continued our new eating habits, and another 18 pounds came off, another doctor's appointment and doing well! Summer came, and I was beginning to enjoy life, I had registered to become a certified life coach with the Certified Coaches Federation. I attained my certificate to coach as well as coach others in addiction!

Mid-summer and I took ill again, losing my balance, I was to experience full-on dizziness, fainting and dropping to the floor started to occur. Crap I was scared to death, as was my partner. Off to emergency, not once. but several times. A battery of tests began again, and this time, my heart was suspect. As time would have it, another reduction in blood pressure medication and test results from a stress cardiogram came back negative! Late summer came and turned into an early fall trip up to Orillia, where Robert J. Moore was hosting the Magnetic Entrepreneur Mastermind weekend! I entered the weekend with no expectations and had the pleasure of meeting fellow authors with a desire to share their stories in this collaborative book, *Breaking Free*! Alan, Brittany, Stephine, Sameh, Ronda, Corey, Charlene, Dr. PPP, Preeti and myself rounded out the Mastermind attendees. There were several breakthroughs on that glorious weekend, and because I am an empath, *I was ready to do justice for some of my new family!* I know and understand that people were open and vulnerable to the process. We all survived the weekend with a new appreciation for life on life's terms, new friends and a renewed zest for life and curiosity to continue to move forward! Imagine! Me! An Author!

As life would have it, after the Mastermind event, we arrived home, and within' a day or so, our seven-year-old grandson had emergency surgery, and we were called from home again. We ended up staying with our son and his family, taking turns visiting our little man in the hospital. By now, I'm a full-blown certified coach, and I want to spread my wings! The beautiful thing about working for yourself and being a coach means I can connect with my clients anywhere in the world. I have an internet connection. In the meanwhile, I was to attend another mastermind with my wife in Toronto in early October. Another tragedy was unfolding; I was to lose my stepson to addiction at 46 years of age. This was the same son who threatened to kill me after leaving his mother, and now ten years later, he lost his life to this horrific addiction of alcohol and drugs. All I could do is mourn from a distance as so much bad blood had distanced us. A week or so later, our nephew had a horrible motorcycle accident. Jordan smashed his body so severely he was airlifted from Kitchener to London, Ontario. He is recovering slowly, and long-term damage to his mind and body is undetermined at this time.

Finally, after all of the difficulties, the summer had brought. I am on track to a much healthier lifestyle. Ronda and I have adopted and love our plant-based meal direction. I have lost a total of 64 pounds, I exercise regularly, mostly walks and beginning soon re-introducing light weights to regain some of my muscle mass again, I have weaned from 15 prescriptions to four as of writing this story! I have created a Men's Health Group for the North Huron and South Bruce counties, and it operates once a month every second Tuesday. I have collaborated with another coach, and we have a recovery retreat planned for the new year of 2020! I am also a contributing columnist for the Lucknow Sentinel (distribution of 1700) Exciting times indeed!

I have recovered, yet again and I continue to engage in personal development and share my experience, strength and hope with others to inspire and make permanent life-changing directions for both myself and my clients. None of this would have been possible without the energy, prayers, and gifts of love, light and energy being sent my way. It inspires me to help others to be a version of their best selves. I continue to do this important work in love and gratitude.

My favourite quotes this year, 2019.

"Choose your friends wisely, show me your top 5 friends, and I'll show you your future"
Robert J. Moore

"Don't waste time looking for your purpose in life. Go out and create it!"
Alan Wade

"I know that I am NOT a burden or a waste of space, but a beautifully complicated person who has gone through hell and back. I still keep on going, and for once, it's not because I feel I have no choice, for the first time, it's because I want to!"
BW. Lamey

"Do I want to become bitter or better? I choose BETTER! What do you choose?"

Cindy Preston

"I rejoiced as I became my own best friend and started listening to my voice of reason, without negative narcissistic viewpoints that had surrounded me for so many years."
Ronda Lauer

"If you are working on something fascinating that you care about, you don't have to be pushed. The vision pulls you!"
Steve Jobs

"A life without a clear vision is like trying to sail a ship without a rudder."
Melissa Anglin

Alan Brogreen

Alan is an internationally best-selling author, a certified life coach and a family man.

Alan has a strong work ethic through his **Life Coaching / Permanent Life-Changing** as he specializes in human behaviour and Mental Health & Addictions. Some of his core values are *empathy, compassion, integrity, trust, strength, hope, wisdom and the dedication to being a Life-Long Learner.*

Alan has been supporting families and individuals in Mental Health and Addictions with high success rates for over 20 years. He has proven techniques, programs and methods that have assisted people in their recovery and improved lives. He provides people in need the proper support they can count on!

Alan can be reached at
(p) 519-513-4776
(E) alan.brogreen@outlook.com
Alan Brogreen on Facebook
Alan Brogreen on YouTube
Alan Brogreen at LinkedIn
www.tameYourDragonsCoaching.com

Overcoming Shame

by B.W. Lamey

Shame can be a painful emotion caused by the consciousness of guilt, shortcomings, or improper behaviour (irregularities, flaws in one's self due to negative role models, to name a few). Shame is such a powerful energy, yet we treat it like it is nothing more than an easy means to an end. Shame can literally change a person's entire life, causing a lifetime of yo-yo diets, bad relationships, weak or low self-esteem, and a sense of not being deserving of the good things in life. It can lead to anxiety and depression, a sense of never being good enough.

There is such a broad sense of failure that haunts someone who hasn't been able to conquer the shame they have felt. It can start at a young age, in adulthood, or in a relationship. No one is immune to the feeling of shame, and the closer the person that did the shaming is to you, the harder it is to overcome. Most people have been shamed and or have shamed someone at some point in their life, oftentimes without even knowing it. Do most people even know or understand what shame is or what it means to shame someone and the negative impact it can have on a person?

From my experience, most don't have a full understanding of either shame or guilt. Often people believe they are one and the same, and confuse the two. However, they are, in fact, not the same at all. I was one of the many who truly didn't know what shame and guilt were because I never was taught what they truly mean or how damaging shame can be to someone. So what is the difference between them? The feeling of guilt is your response to a mistake you have made, which leads you to want to better yourself and fix your mistake. Shame involves an intense and painful focus on one's self in negative ways, "Something is wrong with me." Guilt can lead a person to want to fix their mistakes and better themselves, whereas shame will lead the person to dive deeper into mental despair, causing mental disorders to intensify and can even destroy one's self-worth and self-esteem.

It wasn't until I started learning about "core beliefs" that I finally learned what shame really was. I was, in fact, feeling shame, not guilt, for a lot of things that I had no control or power over at all. I had been researching CPTSD (Complex PTSD is a type of post-traumatic disorder that comes from experiencing trauma at an early age, or trauma that lasted for a long time, rather than just one single event acting as a trigger. Most frequently, CPTSD affects people who've faced long-term physical or emotional trauma, such as sexual abuse, repeatedly witnessing violence, or being kidnapped. It's thought that someone is more likely to develop complex PTSD if the trauma occurred at an early age or lasted for a long time, they were harmed by someone close to them, that escape or rescue were unlikely, or they have experienced multiple traumas.)

I kept seeing the phrases "core beliefs" and "negative belief systems" until I finally took the time to research shame and guilt. I learned that negative self-beliefs can lead not only to self-shaming and low self-esteem, but they have been linked to depression, anxiety and suicide. I carried that shame with me for over 20 years without even truly knowing it. This lack of knowledge was very costly to me and my family. I personally feel that we should all know and understand what shame and guilt really are and how shame can impact not only ourselves but those around us. I had been shaming people without even knowing it until I learned what shame really was. I had spent years believing the negative core beliefs that had been instilled in me as a means to keep me under my parent's control.

Even after I moved away and cut them off, I was still struggling with all the shame and carrying it with me was keeping me from being who I wanted to be, as well as who I was called to be. I wouldn't fully come to accept this until I was finally pushed to my breaking point. I didn't know it then, but all the shame and pain from my childhood was about to erupt. I would end up becoming overcome by the shame that I had unknowingly been living with all those years. My core beliefs were that I was broken and a burden, not worth loving or wanting. I truly believed I was nothing.

That is how powerful and impactful shame can be. Shortly after finding out I had CPTSD, I experienced an episode of psychosis in which I tried to kill myself by overdosing on sleeping medication. This resulted in me staying in the hospital for eight days. The time that I was there, I made it my goal to find out what was behind all this self-hate and why I was convinced that I was worthless and a burden. I reached out to the cognitive therapist about core beliefs and how to change them to positive ones. I knew if I didn't figure out what was behind it all and change it that I would end up dead, I am only here today because my husband was fast enough in getting me help before the medications fully hit my system and my body started to shut down.

During one of the many talks I had with the therapist, he told me about a few books that could help me understand everything better and help me grasp what was going on mentally and why I felt the way I did about myself. As soon as I was released from the hospital, I when on a hunt for the books the therapist told me about as well as some meditation books.

I was raised in a very strict and toxic environment. My household was centred on my parent's methodology and ideals from the born again Christian religious mythology. Shaming us was how they kept us all aligned and loyal. The thoughts we had, the actions we did were things to be ashamed about. They taught us that God was always judging us and that we had to follow the flock like sheep. Our father was hardly ever around because of work, and when he was home, he was always "fixing" things, which left our mentally ill mother who has Munchausen by proxy, among other mental disorders, as our main caregiver.

My mother shamed me for my personality, and how I acted as a person, every chance she got and my sister happily joined in. One moment of shaming that I know impacted me greatly was when my sister told me that I was a disappointment to my parents because I was a tomboy, I was never girly enough and that I was a boy trapped inside a girl's body. She said that was the reason I didn't know how to be a girl and that I was a mistake.

I tried to change and hide who I was and what I liked. I went so far as to let a friend put makeup on me and dress me in girly clothes. I walked down the stairs thinking to myself that my parents would be happy with me that I looked like a girl is supposed to, they would be so glad that I was trying not to act like a tomboy. I don't think I have ever been as wrong as I was that day. The moment my mother saw me, she got upset and yelled at me that I looked like a whore! "If you go out looking like that, you're asking for something bad to happen to you."

This belief that you must have done something wrong for bad things to happen to you was ingrained into me at a very young age. The times I was sexually assaulted left me feeling like I must have done something deeply wrong to be having this happen to me. Shame led me to believe that I deserved what was happening and what was being done to me, no matter how bad it was or how little control I had. "Spare the rod spoil the child" was taken to the extreme by my mother. The smallest of mistakes would result in an assault of being shamed.

My mistake was allowing verbal and emotional abuse to impact my life so drastically that I still, to this day, struggle with feelings of worthlessness and shame. I still struggle against depression and suicidal thoughts; even with all that I have learned and all the therapy I have had, I still struggle with shame. I was never taught about mental health or self-care in a logistical or realistic way. My mother taught me to fear mental illness because those who suffered from it had to have done something ungodly to deserve it; that it was the result of not being right with God.

All of this would lead me to believe that every bad thing that happened to me must have been because I wasn't good enough; I was a mistake and an unwanted burden. I was only seven years old the first time I remember having an overwhelming desire to die, wanting to kill myself. I remember that I was far more scared of what my parents would do if they found out I was having dark thoughts than of the dark thoughts themselves. I wondered if they found out, what would they do to me? Would they disown me or send me away to a mental hospital? Would they care or believe me if I told them? I was too afraid of what would happen if I told them that I kept it to myself for a very long time. My parents are clueless, until one day, my mother hacked into my social accounts and found out I had been struggling with self-harm.

I was born into an environment and raised with shame being used against me. However, I have learned that shame is simply a tool used by some to force their own rules and viewpoints on others. It is not my shame, it is theirs, their rules are not mine to follow or break, and their shame is not mine to own or carry. It is theirs, and I am no longer allowing it to drag me down or hold me back. I have been focusing on learning to tell when I feel shame versus guilt.

I now recognize when I feel shame, when I act out of character, when I act in anger instead of love and when my mental illnesses are triggered. I was so sure for the longest time that I simply got what was coming to me, that I would let my shame drag me down into a spiral of depression and pain that nearly cost me my life. But now, I can forgive myself; I can let go of the shame and learn from it instead of letting it control me. I am only human; we all make mistakes and letting shame control me was one of my biggest challenges, but I am choosing to learn from my shame, and I am no longer held back by it.

Here are the actions I have taken to overcome shame:

1) I have accepted that I cannot change the past and the way I was raised

2) I have realized that I am not responsible for the negative actions of others who are, or are not, mentally ill

3) I have refused to dwell on the hurt I endured, and have released it

4) I have now been able to identify the feelings that contributed to my problems:'GUILT: made a mistake, deep desire to correct and do better, versus SHAME: I am a mistake (this one is huge!), efforts to correct feeling useless, which also includes feelings of sadness, anxiousness,

remorsefulness, sadness, being overwhelmed, depressed, isolated, a failure and not loveable

5) I have assessed my Core Beliefs that I was never good enough, not worthy, why try?

6) I have changed my Core Beliefs by:

- research, learning what my core beliefs are and how to adjust them and make positive lasting change,

- realizing that I am worthy, can have positive self-esteem, be happy, not burdened, be positive and goal-oriented, and make positive lasting life changes

- reflection, that I have the ability to enact permanent change, become more loveable, to establish connections with friends and family and to remove negative thoughts

- being vulnerable enough to ask for help, obtaining help from my husband and children, a Psychiatrist, which involves trust, CBT therapy, meditation, lifestyle change and coaches

These are the areas I am still working on:

1) Forgiving my parents

2) Ensuring my children understand something of what I have been through

3) Building a support network to help me cope in tough times

4) Becoming an Empath – one who experiences the emotions of others

I have come a long way on this difficult road to recovery from shame and would like to encourage you to reach out to me if you are struggling as I was. Please know that this can be overcome, and your life can be so much better! I would like to recommend five ways to help initiate silencing your own feelings of shame.

1. Bring your shame into the light. As a person who is suffering from shame it doesn't seem to make sense to do this; however, the less we talk about it, the more power it possesses over us. Acknowledge it and speak to trusted people in your life. Their empathy will help keep it in check, as well as offer options of how to best deal with it.

2. Untangle what you are feeling. Learn to deeply identify the difference between guilt and shame, in addition to humility or embarrassment. Listen to your inner thoughts and define them as what they are. Take the time to analyze your thoughts and know for sure what message they are delivering.

3. Separate what you "DO" from what you "ARE." If we put our value on what we have to offer our loved ones, friends, or co-workers, we may retreat to feeling shame when our contribution isn't accepted, *i.e.*, "I'm such an idiot," or "I will never be good enough for..." One can become a slave to the performance approval requirements of shame. By doing this, the control of our happiness is in someone else's hands. If we can learn to separate the soul-crushing response of believing this is who we are, from a sense of disappointment in something we have done, it gives us permission to be creative and flourish within ourselves, and it's okay if everyone doesn't approve. It returns our identity and self-worth.

4. Recognize triggers. Insecurities are a prime area where we default to shame. Try to identify what is causing your feelings in the moment. For women, it's often physical appearance; for men, it's being perceived as weak. Rather than deal with these, ban them from your life and fully embrace who you are rather than a false belief of who you believe you should be.

5. Reach out and make connections. For you, it may be family or friends. Maybe it is a higher power; whoever you reach out to, it lets you know you are not alone. It is okay to accept yourself. Prevent the disconnect that shame itself inflicts upon us. You may find yourself saying more often that you aren't so bad, others have experienced worse, and eventually, you may be able to bring yourself to a place, like me, that you can offer insights of how you overcame.

B.W. Lamey

Published Author of the book: *How a Goat Saved my Life - Never Underestimate a Goat*

Contact Info:
You can reach Brittany at: BrittanyLamey@gmail.com or at her Facebook Page:
https://www.facebook.com/MommaDragon88/

THE LEAD™ TECHNIQUE
by Sameh Hassan

Knowledge is power, and the more you learn, the more you earn. I read this statement earlier in my life, and it has fundamentally changed everything I do. So, pat yourself on the back; you did a good thing by reading this book, and you have made it to this chapter!

Would you agree that time and energy are the two most important resources that you cannot afford to waste? If you agree with me on this, I promise that reading this chapter will be worth your valuable time.

I am going to show you how to conduct your evaluation to figure out how to select the right digital marketing consultant who would help you take your business to the next level. You will discover the easy way of finding out how you can hire and partner with the right expert to get you what you want.

My name is Sameh Hassan; I am the only digital marketing consultant who uses the LEAD™ technique.

L stands for Learning about your business to recommend the right solutions for you;

E stands for Excellent quality leads delivered to your website every single hour;

A stands for Accelerate business growth using my strategies; and,

D stands for Doubling your leads without increasing your marketing budget!

I believe that a successful digital marketing consultant should be able to answer the following six questions:

1. How will the business be able to sell online?
2. How will you differentiate and market your product or services?
3. How will you persuade the target audience to take action and buy products and services?
4. What is the right strategy that would enable your business to grow at this stage?
5. How can you leverage social media to get more people interested in the business?
6. How can you measure the progress toward your goals using KPIs – key performance indicators?

These are basically what I believe are crucial questions for any business owner, chief marketing officer, marketing manager, or any manager when hiring a digital marketing consultant to help their business expand online.

I have been known for being one of the few digital marketing experts, who can explain complicated concepts, in a simple way, to help business owners, CEOs, directors, and marketing managers make decisions with more confidence when it comes to digital marketing and business.

My clients say that my LEAD™ technique enables and empowers them to accelerate their business growth, get them more leads, and maximize their revenues even with a limited marketing budget! I want to share with you a story about how a recent client of mine used my LEAD™ technique that turned his new business into an amazing success.

A client of mine, who started a café in Toronto a few years ago, wanted to establish a customer base while launching a new brand in a new location. He had been working for a successful international coffee company. He wanted to combine his expertise with his passion for providing better customer service and his vision to make every customer happy. Although this new brand had limited resources, I was able to bring them 10,000 customers in only one year of launching the business, and now they are expanding by opening a new branch. They also started to receive requests to franchise. I have installed a system that can generate new leads to the café using the power of social media, then intelligently establish communication with the customers based on their behaviour after their first visit to the café.

Would you like to get a similar result for your local business? If your answer is yes! please check: www.TheLEADTechnique.com

As you can see, the LEAD™ technique ensures that your success in digital marketing is imminent. I have used the same technique to help one of the top digital marketing agencies generate a successful Google Ads campaign for large corporations in different industries. The digital marketing agency was very glad that they used this technique to ensure that their large accounts are "wowed" and to ensure they are keeping them for another year. These were clients who work in health care, properties, vacation homes, airlines, private investments, banking, insurance, and wellness industries. The digital operation director was amazed by how using the LEAD™ technique transformed their results for their clients and set them up to beat all their competitors who wanted to acquire these accounts. For more information about the LEAD™ technique, visit www.TheLEADTechnique.com.

Here is the thing people do not see; they see only the nice things about what I have achieved. I was raised with the advice to study hard, get high marks to get into university, and then study hard, get outstanding marks to be able to find a dream job.

Neither of my parents are entrepreneurs. My mother is a housewife who dedicated her life to raising me and my two brothers. My dad is an outstanding professor at the university; he teaches several courses in Accounting and, because of him, I learned the value of money and understanding trends. He was the one who showed me how to learn! Because of that, I have had the desire to become an entrepreneur my whole life. He supported me in challenging times, such as when I made wrong decisions that resulted in financial losses and, more important, that resulted in strengthening my self-confidence in trusting my judgment! He was there for me and helped me get over all the challenges and the failures that I had in my life. All I can say to him is: I love you, Dad, for being a role model of patience, resilience and self-reliance. It's hard to find enough words to acknowledge you for what you have done for me during my whole life. I am a lucky person to have a wonderful father and a great supporting friend like you.

I asked my dad how to become successful in life. He told me that you could achieve this by studying hard and getting high marks and becoming the top of your class, which I did! I graduated at the top of my class with the highest passing marks among my peers. I started a job after graduation selling accounting software to small businesses, but it did not work out well. I was only excited during the interview because of the feeling of happiness after winning the interview process and getting hired. But later on, I did not see this job as my path to feel fulfillment; later on, I discovered that none of these jobs made me feel fulfilled.

I was earning a good income, but I was also spending most of that income. Although I was very successful in my academic career, I was not happy about my success in my working career. I was accepting only the jobs that would pay me the highest possible income at the time, regardless of how I would feel doing these jobs. The reality was, I felt bored and did not have enough passion to make me progress in most of these jobs, especially when I realized that my peers, who spent ten years in these companies were saying what I was feeling at that time. I thought that maybe in time, I would mature enough, and I would get used to the work routine and enjoy it.

Have you been wondering about such things as I was? About how to create an online business, so it pays extra income and, hopefully, one day, would enable me to quit my nine-to-five job? My ultimate dream was to have an online business that would create extra income for me while I am sleeping or something that I can work on one time, and it pays off forever with minimum effort. I understand the concept that we are time traders! We have limited time each year – 2000 hours each year to work!

Sameh Hassan

Sam has been authoring and co-authoring award-winning books in business and digital marketing, including *Affiliate Blogger Guide* and *Digital Marketing For Small Businesses*. He is also actively coaching clients to create information products by converting their knowledge to online classes and collaboration. He has recently launched new training programs for the most significant online market place, udemy.com, and other market places online. The LEAD™ system for local businesses is very affordable, runs on autopilot, and guarantees success for any local business, including restaurants, coffee shops, car service centers, etc.

He has created and operates e-commerce websites for international brands and ranks them organically to be found in search engines like Google and Bing when specific keywords are searched.

He is also the expert behind the scenes for creating successful events; his recent events were in Toronto, Cairo, Dubai, and online too! At these events, he reveals the secrets about how to win at digital marketing that helps business owners understand how to leverage the internet using his unique technique to reach the right audience, persuade them to become customers, and keep them happy for life!

For more information about the LEAD™ technique, visit:

www.TheLEADTechnique.com

This is the time to get a free 20-minute consultation with Sam. Visit:

www.eWebMarketingPro.com

Breaking Free from the Captivity of Limited Thinking
by Charlene Lovegrove

Breaking free is recognizing your potential and escaping the captivity of limited thinking. It is letting go of lies that you have been told, or that you tell yourself about your past, your potential or your passions. Breaking free is the process of changing the way you look at your history. It is looking at the world through possibilities, not limitations. It is within your control to change your self-perception and decide if your past will be the bridge to your potential, or a barrier withholding you from your predestined future.

Our society organizes its citizens within a socially constructed system that is man-made to control movement between societal, economic classes. Movement outside your expected limited potential keeps you subject to a perpetual state of internal and external judgment. Socially constructed labels often are linked to your family's genetic heritage, your unique DNA and your social, economic status at birth. These neat little categories ensure that personal growth and success is limited to the areas society deems appropriate. Once you have accepted a label from society, it becomes your identity, and it requires very little external enforcement or monitoring. These limiting identities often come with an internal fear, shame, and guilt. The intrusion of societal labels and their limiting influences in your life will bind you to the social influences and limit your dreams and potential for the future.

The process of becoming truly free moves you past the oppression and injustices, which leaves you feeling powerless and can manifest itself as a crisis of identity. If you look beyond the societal systems, you will find those humble beginnings and negative societal labels are often what qualities you for the future you have chosen. They do not disqualify you as you may have been taught to believe. Embracing your perfect imperfections allows you to release the compulsion towards societal conformity, to freely embrace your predestined purpose. It is the life struggles within your journey that are behind the passion that forges our directions toward fulfilling our life's perfect plan.

Please journey with me back in time through a life story that at first glance is seemingly riddled with negative influences and unspeakable odds. However, it was the struggles in the journey that created the faith and strength for the future destination. This story begins at Christmas in 1954, which was like many others around the Tyrrell family farm in rural Ontario. The hustle and bustle of preparing for Christmas, as well as keeping up with the demands for turkeys, which was part of Grant's farming operation, kept both Grant and Rhoda on their toes, not to mention the sounds of joy and anticipation from the growing number of children anticipating Christmas. By that time, Grant and Rhoda had given birth to one son, adopted one son and were fostering three additional children all from the same family. Then the telephone call came! Child protective services, knowing Rhoda's heart and her inability to say no, called to request that the Tyrrell family take in just one more child over the Christmas holidays, to provide the child with a good Christmas. Rhoda proceeded to tell then that she would discuss it with her husband and get back to them with an answer as soon as possible. Grant and Rhoda discussed at length their inability to take on anything more at that time, including a child, especially considering the pending holiday and their present circumstance of a full house. After long deliberation, Rhoda prayed and quickly called the Children's Aid Society to say they would be glad to have the little five-year-old girl over the Christmas holiday. After all, what was one more child, and it was only for a short time over the Christmas season. They would give this child a good Christmas!

Having come from a very impoverished and violent home, the shy little girl arrived much amazed by her new surroundings. Her home, after all, did not have even the simplest luxury of hydro or indoor plumbing. Five-year-old Frances Dorothy, with her sandy brown hair and freckles across her nose, stole their hearts immediately. Her brain once wired for connection through the trauma she had experienced had been rewired for self-protection. This timid little child with her head bowed had already had her self-esteem, and her security affected and gaining her trust would prove to be a challenge even for Grant and Rhoda. Rhoda was determined to rebuild her heart so she could once again give and receive love freely. The Christmas season ended, months and then years past and the little girl remained in their home as part of the growing family. Over the years, the family had indicated that they wished to adopt Frances formally, but it was Frances's decision, and she wanted to keep the same last name as her brothers and sister. You see, the family was different on the farm, it was love that defined family, not blood, and Frances knew she was loved. Grant and Rhoda shared the unconditional love and faith that they had living within their hearts and over the years, established a mutually loving relationship with the young child.

The teen years were a turbulent time for this family and their daughter. Like other young ladies her age, Frances sought independence and an outlet to express herself as an individual. It was just before her sixteenth birthday that Frances sprouted wings, stopped attending high school and went out into the world to work and start a life of her own. After only a few months and much dismay with what the world could offer her, the young lady returned home like the prodigal son to receive the unconditional love and acceptance she had come to rely on from her foster parents. Her foster parents welcomed her home with open arms, much like the first day she arrived. The past events were forgotten, and only her future well-being was considered. She had stolen their heart from the first day, and there would always be a place in their home where she could find refuge.

It was not long after she returned home before her foster mother heard rumours of her daughter's condition, an unplanned pregnancy. Rhoda took her daughter to the doctor, and the rumour was confirmed as truth, Frances was pregnant. Receiving this news came with much disappointment and shock to both Grant and Rhoda. Once again, she was to secure their true unconditional love. The news was accepted, the mistake was forgiven, and the plan for how they would handle this situation was put into place. After all, Rhoda was determined that her daughter would be an overcomer. The generational trauma, addictions, incarceration, and poverty that plagued many indigenous children like Frances would not be repeated in their foster children.

The foster parents once again came alongside their daughter and supported her through this challenging situation. Unplanned pregnancies, at this time were uncommon, and to save the family, the humiliation young women were often hidden in secret or the pregnancy terminated. Frances was never criticized or made to feel ashamed about her condition. The Tyrrells knew that although their daughter's child was a surprise to them, the child was created with a plan and purpose. With their strong faith leading them, they came alongside their daughter and helped to ensure the baby arrived safely, and termination was never a consideration.

The plan was for Frances to remain at the farm throughout her pregnancy, and when the baby arrived, it would be put up for adoption to a loving home. As the end of the pregnancy neared and with France underage and still a ward of the courts, the decisions surrounding the delivery were outside of her control. The child protective services and the family doctor made plans to induce labour early to ensure that the child would be delivered before Frances turned eighteen. This would remove any legal right or decision making from the young mother, and she would not need to be consulted about the child's future. Frances was induced as planned and went into labour on her eighteenth birthday. Through divine providence and after many hours of labour, Frances gave birth to a healthy baby the next day, at which time the adoption process began.

Three days had passed since Rhoda's foster daughter had given birth, and the Lord continued to speak to her about the new baby. While reconsidering the decision to place the baby for adoption, Rhoda consulted with her son, who also had been adopted. His reply was simple, "not everyone receives a loving home as I did." Rhoda being a woman of faith, continued to seek the Lord for His will for this child. As divine coincidence would have it when she arrived at the hospital to speak to Frances about the child's future, a pastoral meeting had just concluded. Four pastors were standing in the hall of the Dunnville War Memorial Hospital just down from her daughters' room. Not being a shy woman, Rhoda approached the pastors and shared her dilemma with them. She left the room after praying with the godly men feeling she knew God's will. If her daughter agreed, the child would remain in the Tyrrell family and would be received with open and loving arms.

At that time, it was the practice that if one was to put a child for adoption, you did not see the child, nor were you informed of the gender. The child was quickly whisked away to make the separation easier for the new mother. Adoption was a difficult choice to make, but Frances knew that it was the right thing to do, as, on her own, she could not provide for this new life. Rhoda arrived in the room just as her daughter had received the papers from the nurse to sign, for the adoption of her first-born child. Rhoda asked the nurse to leave so that she could speak to her daughter in private before she was to sign the papers. After many tears of joy, the nurse was summoned back to Frances' room, where she was asked to bring the child immediately to them.

The nurse and the child protection agency were very unhappy about the possibility of allowing the baby to remain with the young mother who had seemingly already started down the same path as her biological mother, who struggled in poverty, with addictions, and had nine children in the foster care system. Frances, after all, was a runaway, had become pregnant outside of marriage at a very young age and had already been before the courts for underage drinking. Frances's indigenous cultural roots, biological family history and years in the foster system set her in the spotlight for scrutiny and judgment from a society that felt she was incapable and ill-equipped to be a mother. Racism, even in its most seemingly benign forms, can shape who you are, and society had decided that this indigenous young lady fit the stereotypical mould, and she would become her mother.

When her foster parents looked at Frances with love, they saw a young woman that deserved a chance to prove she could rise above the circumstances and stereotypes that surrounded her and be a mother with their guidance and support. The child whom they learned was a little girl would not be placed up for adoption. The young lady and the new baby girl were received home to the farm with much fanfare and excitement from her foster parents, brothers, and sisters. Once again, their loving arms were extended to welcome another into their growing family.

Little did Grant and Rhoda know that the decision made that day to enable Frances to keep the girl baby would change the course of all their lives forever. The bond between a parent and child could never be stronger and would never be broken. These three wonderful people within this life story, have all since gone on to their eternal reward. However, Grant, Rhoda, and Frances's legacy of love lives on. Their faith-driven unconditional, non-judgemental love that once received changes you forever.

Now allow me to introduce myself, I am the product of the unplanned pregnancy of a runaway ward of the courts, Charlene Anne born January 31 and the legacy of unconditional love that was given to my mother lives on in me. Many times, over the years, my grandmother would lovingly reminisce about the day she ran into the pastors in the hospital after my birth. With tears in her eyes, she would say, "What would we have ever done without you in our family, you are such a blessing." There was never a time when my grandparents were not at my side when I needed them. My grandmother was my best friend, confidante, pastor and my biggest fan. My grandfather was the active silent type, a man of few words and an excellent example of our heavenly father and the priest of the home. I will be forever grateful for having them in my life as encouragers and faith-filled role models. What I have learned is that it is subjective perceptions that judges people and the events in our lives. We can reject the negative words that we and others use to describe our lives, which influences the way we perceive our role within the world. Despite everything that appeared to be against me when I was born, there was a predestined plan and purpose for my life that was bigger than any of the worldly circumstances. I arrived at just the right time, and although I was a surprise to my mother, there was a plan and a purpose for my life. I was born to the right mother with everything she needed to raise me and eventually met the man of her dreams and created a loving family of her own. I was born into just the right extended family that would accept me as their own regardless of what the world would say, recognizing and investing in my value.

Much like the amazing family that I have have been incredibly blessed to be born into, I chose to use my life to love and serve others. Love is what we have been born with, but it is learned fear and unworthiness that distracts and limits our beliefs and potential. Our spiritual journey to uncover our purpose begins with breaking free from fear and societal prejudices. Do not let the fear of your past experiences distract you from your purpose and the giftings that have been placed within you. You are loved, you have been created with a purpose, break free from the options of others and limiting influences. Move forward with confidence knowing your past has perfectly positioned you for your future.

I am unapologetically me; I am no longer a prisoner constrained by what society or others think about my past or future. The identity crisis created by society has been replaced with the identity I have created for myself. The fear of not assimilating and someone finding out my family history and culture is gone. The light skin colour that I hid my culture behind with shame and guilt, I now recognize as a tool to amplify my voice for those who have had their voices taken away. That person is no longer controlled by humble beginnings or societal labels and has released the need to be perfect, striving for position and relevance. My past struggle has created my current strength, and I am using every event and experience that I have had in the past to help others move into their predestined future. I have broken free from the past, embraced struggles, accepted adversity and faced challenges. The only thing I own in adversity is my response to it, and in the words of my mother, I will do so, "always brave and cheerful." As I look back over my life, I am amazed at the strength and courage of those family members that went before me and how everything leading up to this moment in my life has prepared me for this miraculous journey.

Despite all the different roles I play in this life, the one consistent focus that runs through every aspect of my life is my desire to approach every individual and circumstance with the same unconditional love I have received from my family that chose me at birth and my creator that made me with a purpose to pursue a life of service to others. What I have learned over the years is my life and the work I do is essential and not an accident, much like me. Daily, I mindfully sit across from the hurting, soulfully connected in love, making eye contact with the invisible, helping them to feel worthy to set them free. Life is not a competitive race with winners and losers. Striving for significance in the eyes of the world is a race with no end. The focus on power distracts from what is important, and that's people, connection and love. There is no need to compare yourself with others or to judge yourself to find your value. Your value does not decrease just because of society's inability to see your worth.

Although my life story continues to reveal beautiful new paths, my story has come full circle. God, in His mysterious and wonderful wisdom, allowed me to show a small token of my appreciation to my grandparents for their significant contribution to my life at the time of my grandfather's death. Just as my grandfather was there with open arms to receive me on my journey into this world, making me the person I am today, I was given the privilege of being there with my grandfather to hold his hand in loving appreciation to help to usher him out of this world and into his eternal reward. I am forever grateful!

Charlene Lovegrove

Charlene Lovegrove is the co-author of a national bestseller, and one of the founding members and Corporate Manager of Victim Services of Haldimand Norfolk Mississaugas of the Credit First Nation. The development of strong relationships founded in empathy and compassion are foundational to everything she does personally and professionally. With almost three decades of experience, she oversees programs and services to help individuals and families in the aftermath of crime, tragic circumstances and disaster.

Charlene's formal studies include sociology and theology. Her professional interests in helping others are focused on her accomplishments as a Certified Master Coach Practitioner with Certified Coaches Federation, and as a Pastor with the Pentecostal Assembly of Canada. In addition, she has received certifications as a National Victim Advocate and a National Crisis Responder with the National Organization for Victim Assistance with many specialties. Charlene has extensive experience working alongside and shares her expertise by serving on a variety of humanitarian charities and committees in the areas of homicide, suicide, sudden death, assaults, sexual assault, domestic violence, motor vehicle and fire fatalities, robberies, addictions, hate crimes, anti-human trafficking, and massive-scale disaster.

As a strong advocate of being a learner for life, Charlene is an Applied Suicide Intervention Skills Training (ASIST) Trainer with Living Works and Mental Health First Aid Trainer with Mental Health First Aid Canada. She is also involved in training and speaking engagements in areas of her passion for bringing hope and healing. Some areas of training expertise are crisis intervention, vicarious trauma, resilience, lethality assessment, change management, outcome measures, the neurobiology of trauma, mental health, and addictions.

Charlene's philosophy for life is to surround herself with people who support her to be the best version of herself she can be, and who love her unconditionally when she is not her best.

Magnetic Entrepreneur

RIZE UP
by Corey Phair

Journal entry August 7 2018 "Holy f#ck I feel like shit! I've been eating like shit, no routine and I missed workouts. I was high on Friday, drunk Saturday and high Sunday. I'm depressed as f#ck right now with lots of anxiety! Why is it so f#cken hard for me to be stable? It's obvious that when I eat clean, I have good workouts and don't abuse. I feel much better" This was written by me four days before the last time I got high. If I kept going the way I was, it was just a matter of time before I ended up in jails, institutions or death. Five months after getting clean, I wrote, "I'm starting to realize I was destined for so much more in life. The responses I've gotten from my FB posts, my life experience and role models have all confirmed that I was meant to make a difference in people's lives. I love helping others with mental health and addiction. However, I know I am capable of motivating and inspiring anyone to be their absolute best. No matter what their struggles are in life. F#ck, I feel good!"

February 2013, I was 31 years old and living on base in Petawawa, Ontario. I was part of the military unit 1RCR. I had a wife, two little boys, a good career and some massive goals I was working to achieve. Before I joined the army, I had completed a two year Police Foundations diploma. My plan was to do a three-year contract in the Infantry to beef up my resume to one day be an OPP officer (Ontario Provincial Police), or Bruce Power NRT

(Nuclear Response Team). I was healthy, extremely motivated and happy. Life was good! The day things changed for me, I was in the LAV barn doing vehicle maintenance. I was on top of a light armoured vehicle lifting part of the main gun when something popped in my back. I knew something was seriously wrong, as I felt some of the worst pain of my entire life. I went to the base hospital and was examined by Medical Officer Brown, followed by x-rays. I was told that I had spondylolisthesis at my L4-L5 (slippage of the discs) WO Brown explained to me that I would eventually need surgery and that I should transfer out of the Infantry ASAP. As of that moment, I was put on a TCAT (temporary accommodations or modified duties)

That was the first domino to fall in a chain of events that lead to several very dark years. That injury has caused me chronic pain ever since. This is not like a little boo-boo on the fingertip that heals up after five days. My back pain can be intense! Sometimes it can be crippling. Thank God I have good days and bad days. Because of the way I used to deal with the physical pain, I experienced a lot of mental pain in the form of depression and anxiety. Unfortunately, I took my frustrations out on the ones closest to me. Chronic pain turned me into a miserable prick as it does to many people. My mental pain no longer exists, but my physical pain does and always will. My wife left me and took our kids in April 2014. I can't say that I blame her. I was not easy to live with. Being alone only made things worse. I had my health, a family, and a good career. All of a sudden, it was all gone.

I finished my military contract in June 2014 and then moved back home to Hepworth, Ontario. That's when I started working for a local armoured car company called Gardaworld. This was when I got a new family doctor, and they prescribed the opiate hydromorphone for my pain. These pills were trouble from day one. I still remember the first day I got high on them. I took one as prescribed and then looked at the bottle and wondered what it would feel like to take three more. An hour later, my physical pain, as well as mental pain, was gone.

That is how my addiction started. I would take pills all day long until my bottle was empty. My benders would usually last five or six days. The next week would be hell from the withdrawals — major depression, anxiety, irritability, insomnia, and head and stomach aches. After the withdrawals went away, I would slowly start to feel better day by day. By that point, I was a drug addict. When I was out of pills, all I would think of was getting them and getting high to mask the pain. I would either steal my dad's pills, buy from the street or get drunk in between scripts to tie me over.

Once it was time for a refill, I wouldn't even make it out of the pharmacy parking lot before I downed a handful. I started to crush them up and snort them to get a quicker high. It's incredible how fast my tolerance went up with them. Every time I would run out, I would become suicidal for several days because of how bad my depression got. I never hesitated even once at that point to get high, knowing how low I would get once I ran out. I knew I was going to suffer when the drugs dried up, but at least my physical and mental pain would be gone temporarily. July 2015, my back pain and mental health got so bad, and I had to stop working. Even though my employment was only temporary part-time, I had something in my life. I had a purpose.

Things began to get much worse then. I had nothing to fill my time with. Boredom is very dangerous for an addict. "Idle hands do the devil's work" My pill cycle continued over and over and over. At that point, I had tried just about everything to help deal with my back pain. Physio, massage, chiro, pain clinic, injections and yoga all with very little relief. It was time for surgery.

February 2018, I had a spinal fusion and decompression. After five days in the hospital, my surgeon sent me home with 400 oxys. I remember looking at all the pills after I had my prescription filled and thought three things. 1- Holy shit, that is a lot! 2- I'm going to have some fun and 3- this is going to be trouble. I stayed high for a month straight and then got monthly refills. Once again, the cycle continued. This time, the drugs were more powerful. At this point, I knew I had a serious problem. Sometimes I would grab my pill jar and stare at them, trying to resist the temptation. I'd put the jar down on my counter and walk away only to return two minutes later to swallow a bunch.

Occasionally I would dump some into my hand and resist, put them back on the counter and walk away and come back a minute later and down a bunch. Once in a while, I would put a handful in my mouth and fight it not to swallow. I'd spit them back into the jar and walk away. Minutes later, I'd return and take some. This is the power of addiction.

By that time, I had a new family doctor who cared about my well-being. I was honest with her explaining how I had a problem with oxy's and needed to cut them out. We eventually tapered my dose from 90mg day to 30mg day. Also, my script refill would be on a weekly basis, not a monthly basis. Tuesdays used to be my favourite day of the week. I would show up at the pharmacy at 8:20 am. Ten minutes before it opened. 8:30 hit and I'd go in to top up. As soon as I got out to the truck, I would take all fourteen pills — no pain on those days. Once I finally got off the oxy's, I was abusing lyrica just as much. This was the third time I switched my DOC (drug of choice) The same cycled continued. I went to Emerge several times because I was thinking of suicide. Thank God my kids were in my life!

August 11th, 2018, was the day I changed my life. Three things stand out in my head at that time that impacted me. The first was my DBT (dialectical behavioural therapy). My caseworker gave me a DVD to take home and watch. "Cake" was the movie with Jennifer Anniston. This is a huge comeback story of someone who had very similar problems as I did at the time. My brother is a long-distance runner and was doing a race in Wiarton that day. I was there to cheer him on.

I ran into a buddy who I have done drugs with and partied with in the past. We used to have very similar lifestyles. He was telling me how he had completely turned his life around and is now a trauma counsellor. That was very powerful to see knowing where he had come from. Once my brother finished the race, I said to myself, "why the f#ck am I not doing stuff like this?" That was the moment I had finally had enough.

I was sick and tired of wasting my life. I knew deep down inside of me, and there was huge potential. It was time to stop wasting it. A couple of weeks after my clean date, I wrote out a post on Facebook. There wasn't much thought behind it other than being proud of my accomplishment and wanting to show some close friends that change is possible if you are willing to put in the work. Within minutes of doing that post, my phone started going off with messages from people thanking me for talking openly about my struggles. Some said that I inspired them to make a change in their own life.

I remember thinking, "Wow, this feels good" I kept doing the Facebook posts and kept getting the positive feedback. That is when and how I discovered my passion for helping others. I get a rush every time I help another person. This is my new addiction. I have become obsessed with personal development so I can help serve others. I don't care how far gone someone is. Whether its addiction to drugs or alcohol, mental health, employment, homelessness, or whatever the struggle. If there is a will, there is away. I am living proof that anything is possible if you are will to take full accountability for your life and put in the effort.

I went from rock bottom to rock-solid, and so can you. I am the happiest and most fulfilled I have ever been. I never dreamed that life could be so good. I have invested a ton of time, $ and effort into myself to become my best self. I am now a life coach, personal trainer, speaker and author. I've done DBT (dialectical behavioural therapy)

WRAP (wellness recovery action plan) ASIST (applied suicide intervention skills training) mental health first aid and a four-week intensive pain clinic.

I have read many books, attended seminars and workshops all to help myself and others. I honestly believe that everything happens for a reason, and it serves us. I want my life experience to help make a difference. There have been many life lessons I have learned from my past. Accountability is one of the biggest. When I was suffering, I always had an excuse for everything. My chronic pain, depression, anxiety, other people, my childhood all held me back because I wouldn't take responsibility for my life.

August 11 2018 was the day I looked myself in the mirror and realized that I was the cause of all my problems. Nothing will ever change if you play the blame game and are stuck in a victim mentality. You must take full accountability if you want your life to change. My confidence and core beliefs have completely changed, as well. I used to have many limiting beliefs about myself. Many of these came from my childhood. I know for a fact that anything is possible if you are willing to commit. Now there isn't a single negative core belief in my head. Only empowering ones. Because of this, my confidence and self-esteem are through the roof. Evidence of this is public speaking. Like most of the general public, I used to be terrified of speaking in front of a group. As of now, my biggest crowd is 70 people.

I love public speaking now! There is no better way to make a powerful impact on so many at once. Insecurity used to rule my life. Now, because of my confidence and empowering core beliefs, I am very secure in who I am. I used to have a huge ego, and that's one reason I suffered for so long. I honestly thought that I could handle my mental health and addiction all on my own. Obviously not. Ego holds so many good people back from greatness. In my eyes, we are all equal. When I became humble, I became teachable. Honesty, open-mindedness and willingness are three tremendous words in recovery. If you are fat, you are fat. If you are skinny, you are skinny. If you are an asshole, you are an asshole. You need to own that and be honest with yourself. Once you do that, only then do you become open and willing to try new things.

I used to pass judgement all the time on others. I know now why I did that and why so many others do it. A judgemental person passes their insecurities on to another to make themselves feel better. I feel pretty good about myself and don't need to do that anymore. I have cut out all the negative or toxic people from my life. I refuse to let other people's bullshit bring me down anymore. The ones I do associate with, help bring out the best in me, as I do them. You need to get rid of those people who weigh you down.

I now know what my purpose in life is. That is to help make this world a better place because of my experience. I am very passionate about helping others and get to do it every day. This is one huge reason why my life is so amazing. You have to have something in your life you are passionate about. Stop shooting yourself in the foot with your excuses. You are right where you are in life right now because of you. ANYTHING is possible if you are willing to put in the work. I am living proof of that. Stop wasting your potential and caring what the world thinks of you. Life is short. Every day that passes gets us one step closer to the end. Make them count! "Character can not be developed in ease and quiet. Only through experience of trial and suffering can the soul be strengthened, ambition inspired, and success achieved."

If you are looking to live life to the fullest and would like to do some coaching with me, check out my Facebook page or website. Or contact me by phone or email.

Corey Phair

Facebook page- Rize Up
Website- rizeup.ca
Email- **coreyphair@live.ca**

Spirit of a Wounded Child
By Preeti Chopra

Have you ever wondered how you arrived at where you're at in life, right at this very given moment? It's an accumulation of every single experience and stimulus you've ever encountered.

I didn't have an excellent start in life, as I entered this world when my mother was only seven and a half months pregnant, which made me a premie baby. I was born in Bombay, India, where there was a massive shortage of doctors and nurses at that time, and one had to improvise a lot to survive.

A major artery in my right ankle broke upon entry and the artery needed to be held together for about three and a half days. Both my mother and my aunt Rosy, who was a military nurse, took twelve-hour alternating shifts, holding the artery together, to make sure the artery healed without any serious complications or infections... Two and a half weeks after this horrendous ordeal, I developed pneumonia, and my weight dropped from five pounds to two and a half pounds. My mother told me that I fit curled up into the palm of her hands, the size of a bird and she didn't think that I was going to survive. I was certainly a fighter, and I thrived with every breath that I took.

My fathers' family-owned gold and silver knitting mills and sewed the most beautiful designs onto sarees and my father was a travelling salesman who sold them to earn a living,

Our family lived modestly in a three-room flat on the upper level of a stone building. A well was located in the center of the courtyard and the entry to our home by a metal spiral staircase. I had three older siblings, one sister, two elder brothers and one younger brother who joined our family after I turned four. We all shared a family bedroom, which consisted of three bunk beds and a crib with a large kitchen. There was a common bathroom facility located just outside our flat.

One day, as everyone was taking an afternoon nap, I sat on the veranda, singing lullaby songs to my Indian dolls as I brushed their long beautiful hair. Suddenly, I was carried off into a dark corner of the kitchen, by our servant man, who'd placed a gigantic lollipop in my hand and attempted to rape me. I was only three years old, and thankfully my father heard the sounds of my squealing, flew open the sliding wooden door and saved me from being hurt. My father beat up this man and fired him on the spot, threatening his life if he were ever to come back to our home. That day my father became my hero, and I wanted very much to please him and remain a good little girl in his eyes.

As I sat one seat from the window aboard a gigantic plane, they called a jumbo jet, I turned around to eavesdrop on a conversation my parents were having. They were talking about why we had to leave Bombay in such a hurry. It was quite alarming to hear that our relatives had disapproved of my father and mother being married. You see, my mother was born an Anglican Christian, and my father was born a Suni Muslim. My mother was exactly one year older than my father, and she was his English tutor. That's how they first met back in college. Even though they had eloped and gotten married ten years earlier, the family members on my father's side were angered by the union. They had threatened to kill all of us and refused to let us live in peace. My parents, with the help of a few trusted family members, were able to escape unscathed. The look of sadness poured out of my mothers' eyes as she turned to look at us and realize that she was leaving all that she ever knew behind. My relatives on my mother's side were sponsoring us, and they were to meet us at the Toronto International Airport upon our arrival.

Everything started wonderfully, and my aunts' families even celebrated Christmas with us in March because we didn't get our travel visas till then. I was made Mother Mary in a play, and my eldest brothers were the wise men, my sister, the angel of Bethlehem and my baby brother, who was only a one-year-old played sweet baby Jesus.

We all got along quite nicely and enjoyed each others' company with jovial laughter, excellent food and drinks, Christmas carol singing by our relatives and presents for all.

My parents bought a beautiful house on Waverly Blvd near Kew Beach. It was the best house we ever lived in, and we had a wading pool right outside our back gate, with blackberry bushes lined up in a row beside the public library, where we'd go picking and eating the blackberries and go home with our faces covered in purple fruit juice. I loved riding my tricycle on the rolling hills of the park and laying on the beautiful sandy beach. There we would swim for hours and enjoy the sounds of the birds chirping and the beautiful blossoming flowers along the landscape.

Then about four months after we immigrated to Canada, my father got sick with typhoid and was never the same again.

One day before my sixth birthday, we were all sitting at the dinner table, getting ready to eat when my mother asked, "Who is going to sleep in Papas bed tonight?" I thought that was a strange question, as I'd never heard my mother ask that question ever before. My father pointed to me, said my birth name and stated that I would be sleeping in his bed that night. A sudden feeling of fear came over me, and as soon as I finished eating my supper, my mother instructed me to wash up, brush my teeth, put my pj's on and lay in my fathers' bed. Even though it was still light outside, I decided to go to sleep quickly, so I could get rid of this feeling of doom that had crept into every available space in my stomach.

I fell off to sleep to be awoken by my father whispering something to me. As my eyes opened to the lamplight shining from the bedside, I smelled an unusual odour as my father ordered me to perform a lewd act. Frightened to death by the sound of my father's unfamiliar voice, I felt like puking at the gruesome sight of his body part pressed up against my lips. My body was paralyzed by fear, and my spirit instantly jumped out of my body. I stood there helplessly watching the terror on my face as I was forced to do the unthinkable.

My child's spirit and my innocence, in that very moment, were destroyed. I felt dirty, tainted and utterly despicable.

Even though I was only five and a half years old, my spirit knew that what was being done to me was wrong and was against God. My father told me countless times that if I ever told anyone about this, he would kill me and cut up into tiny little pieces, place me into a black garbage bag and throw me away, and nobody would ever know. I believed my father. His words echoed in my mind as I lay in bed, praying for my death. I didn't know what I did wrong to create this monster that lived in our home and not under my bed.

My father would pull me out of bed at night at least once a week for years (except never in his holy month, those thirty days I was completely safe) while all the family members were sleeping. If my mother woke up and asked him why he was calling for me, he would say that he wanted me to press on his feet or his back, and that would be a reasonable answer for my mother, who would then go back to sleep. The rare time that I would get out of being abused was when he'd fall asleep while I pressed on his feet. I would press lightly once I knew he was sleeping, and then I'd tiptoe out of his room and escape the ordeal that night.

He'd often keep me home from school, violating me before I left. Each time he turned into someone else, with a look of lust in his eyes, as I know now, and of pure evil.

How could a man who prayed so many times a day have the urge to violate a child, let alone his own child? What was I doing to cause this to happen to me? Was I just a bad seed, a naughty girl that deserved this type of punishment?

I prayed to God vigilantly, begging for Him to take me back. I didn't want to be here, and I was living the biggest lie. How did I pray to God and strive always to do good deeds but not be able to stop my father from doing these horrible indecent acts to me? I was more terrified of my father than I was of God.

Many times, I had spiritual things happen after a painful experience with my father. As I lay in bed, weeping quietly so I wouldn't wake my mother or sister, I felt an enormous amount of hatred that I had accumulated against myself. I begged God to return me to heaven and then, I tried hard to hold my breath, smothering my face into the pillow desperately aching to end my own life.

Have you ever had to cry silently? It's not easy to do when your body is aching from the torture of the pain you just went through.

Sometimes I would see white light energy spiralling in my room, flooding the air with love and starlight. The waves of energy would appear out of nowhere and fill the darkness with a gentle floating rhythm. I felt the presence of God in the bedroom, and it was only then that my tears stopped flowing down my face. I was mesmerized by God and the love flowing through me in this magical light. This white beaming light would lull me to sleep, and I would have the best sleep ever when these lights appeared.

I failed kindergarten, and I got the strap for saying the "f" word to my teacher as my new friends instructed me because I didn't know one word of English. Being that my mother was an English teacher in India, my mother put her foot down and told my dad that we needed to learn to speak English in our home. Of course, there was a massive fight for power, and my mother won that battle.

The next six years of my life at home became a series of beatings, night trauma and religious extremism.

Every household has a black sheep, I'm told. In our family, we had two black sheep, my brother and I. My older brother, who looked identical to me, was sent to a group home when he was only 11 years old because he was caught skipping school and smoking marijuana in a back alleyway. Personally, I think my father got rid of him so he could violate me in peace. My eldest brother was a geek and was always studying. Therefore, he was never going to see what my father was doing to me, in the middle of the night. My sister was busy getting her beauty sleep and being the bossy sister she enjoyed being. My baby brother was just that, a cute baby.

My father ruled the household like Hitler, with my sister being hailed second in command. My mother surrendered her power to my sister, always asking her what, where, when, and how we should do anything. I don't know why mum gave up her power.

When he lectured us about God, religion and his spiritual travels, I had a hard time paying attention and staying awake. I think deep down, I knew he was a disgrace to his religion, and all his praying was such a farce.

I desperately wanted to be in my fathers' good books so, I worked hard at doing daily household chores, cooking meals for the family with my sister and delivering the Sears flyers once a week. From twelve years to sixteen, I delivered 185 of The Toronto Star newspapers with my little brother's help, six days a week. We also attended Sunday school, had to do school projects, religious homework and pray five times a day. I always felt sleep deprived because there were so many responsibilities put on us at a very young age.

The most fun I ever had as a child was at school recess, where I would play like an average child. I'd sing some good and some bad songs on my way to school, play street ball hockey, climb trees with my brothers, play hide-and-seek with my baby brother and his friends, or do my own thing when no grownups were home.

Around the age of twelve, my mother started taking us to watch Indian movies in the theatre because we forgot all five languages (Urdu, Hindi, Gujrati, Marati and Punjabi) that we spoke before we came to Canada. English is my sixth language, not my first.

Then with my $1.50 allowance, I saved up for an Indian music album. I would dress up in my Indian clothes, play the Indian dance music and prance around like a Bollywood movie star all around the dining room table. I knew all the dance movements, and I could do the hand gestures and the shy facial expressions so well. Oh my, did I ever have fun! I loved to laugh, and I laughed so hard I didn't care that it was against my religion to laugh hard from the pit of my belly. I didn't give a damn. I needed a vice and singing in Hindi and dancing was mine.

My father didn't realize that he moulded me to be abused by men outside our home. I was a tomboy. I would sometimes get touched inappropriately during an intermission in a dark corridor, connecting the elementary school with a middle school, where the boys and I played ball hockey at lunchtime. It was another paralyzing moment that didn't last too long that I was able to bear because I thought it was normal for the male species to do these kinds of things to me. One boy picked me up and put me on the back banana seat of his bike and drove me down to the beach, where he had made cardboard shed. He forcefully pulled off my pants and raped me. As I was fighting to keep my pants on, I kept repeating to him. "My Papa does this to me too! My Papa does this to me too!" He was too intoxicated with lust to even pay attention to my plea.

I grew up with many more disturbing things that happened to me by my fathers' hands. At the tender age of 18, my father sold me to an abusive refugee for his freedom. I didn't know I was sold. It was made to look like a kidnapping after my first day of a summer school course. It was such a brilliant plan and worked out in both my father's and the refugee's favour.

At the age of twenty-three, I escaped the clutches of this highly irresponsible alcoholic and poker addicted refugee husband while pregnant with my third child. He squandered all my hard-earned money, and we were getting ready to be evicted from a place where he gambled away three months' worth of rent money. My best option was to break out of the prison I was in, and raise my children on my own. I got into a shelter and found government housing, gave birth to my child and got varicose vein surgery. I got a college education, met a Scottish man and fell in love, or so I thought. I had two children with him and decided to cut him loose because he wasn't an ideal husband nor an appropriate father to our children.

Finally, when my mind was at peace and no longer battling to survive each day, I spent many months reflecting on my past. My heart was genuinely grateful that I survived such horrendous circumstances, but my self-esteem took a beating. I chose to forgive every person who violated me and shed the victim label and decided to become victorious.

I broke free from the paradigms of my past. I carried the shame for 50 years that was not mine to own. Throughout my journey, my unshakeable faith and deep love for the Lord brought me through my darkest times. I chose to forgive my father as I found out years later that he was also abused sexually as a child. Perhaps he thought he loved me, and I waited till he passed in 2009 before I dared to begin healing my body, mind and soul.

I am a total of all my experiences, and I can look at the woman in the mirror and know that I am grateful for the beautiful heart that God placed inside of her. I am not tainted nor damaged goods as I once thought I was. I'm ready to serve by teaching people how to rise above the adversities that they may be facing. I'm willing to show people how to develop unshakable faith through the power of their thoughts. And how to forgive from the tender parts of their souls genuinely.

Preeti Chopra

Preeti Chopra is a courageous, warm-hearted and spirited woman. She travelled through the dark tumultuous seasons of life, to discover the strength of her unshakeable faith, the power of true forgiveness and having the tenacity, born of desperation, to conquer the demons of her past.

A serious car accident in 2013 brought on a spiritual revelation which caused Preeti to leave her mortgage career behind. She embarked upon an entirely different adventure, unleashing the power of her voice, that for many years had been silenced by those who were responsible for her safety.

In 2016, Preeti was discovered by an ex-child soldier turned recording artist, who encouraged her to speak her story of resilience, faith and forgiveness to the world. She was invited onto the We Want Peace stage during a concert to speak about the way she was able to forgive her father, for the atrocities he made her endure during her childhood.

Today, Preeti is a mother to five wonderful children, a certified speaker, a published author, and personal life coach.

She is using her story to awaken people to the desires of their souls. They learn how to reignite their passions to take consistent actions and live into a future by their own design.

THE CELEBRITY COACH
by Dr. Pravin P. Patel (#DRPPP)

Hello! Amen! Ameen! Namaste! I am "The celebrity Guru" award-winning author of the book "You *are the Celebrity*." I am the #1 international bestseller and the Magnetic Entrepreneur award-winning author of the book "*Magnetic Entrepreneur – A Personality That Attracts*." I am the Magnetic Entrepreneur award-winning author & International bestseller of the book "*Magnetic Entrepreneur Mastermind*." I am the Guinness Book of the World Record author of the book "*Magnetic Entrepreneur World-Renowned*". I am the marathon man who ran 8+ marathons in my life by God's grace and your blessings. I am The Himalayas Guru, who is climbing the Everest, the Himalayas by May 31, 2020, by God.s grace and your blessings. If the Celebrity Guru can write, so can you. If the Marathon Man can run, so can you. If the Himalayas Guru can climb, so can you. Life is the Movie. You are the Celebrity. Life is the Celebration. You are the Celebrity. Life is the Marathon. You are the Marathoner. Life is the Book. You are the Author. Life is the Mountain. You are the Mountainer. I served in the Canadian Army as an engineer by God's grace and your blessings.

A Coach is the one who can bring you from darkness to the light. A Coach helps you sail form sea of sameness to the island of individuality. A Coach helps you to achieve your wildest dreams. A Coach is the one who is already where you would love to reach. When you are in a fog, it's foggy. A

Coach can bring you out of a fog. You can save time, money and energy by having the right coach in your life. Successful people are successful because they have several coaches to take care of different aspects of their lives. To awaken the spirituality within, you need a spiritual Guru. To have amazing health, you need a health coach. To have peace of mind in your life, you need a life coach. To add sparkle to your relationship with your loved ones, you need a relationship coach. To take care of finances, you need a financial coach. During your school life, you have teachers. During your college life, you have professors. How come you don't have any coaches when you are living your life? You can learn a lot from your coaches to have peace of mind. You get punished during your school and college life if you copy during the exam. In the game of life, you copy your coach's proven system to have peace of mind.

You put your coach's wisdom into action after learning from your coach. Every game has a coach. Every successful person has coaches. How about you? Why not learn from someone else's mistakes so you can save time, money and energy? A Coach is going to bring you to the next level. A Coach is going to stretch you, so you can achieve impossibilities. A Coach is going to teach you "I AM POSSIBLE" instead of IMPOSSIBLE. You can sail the ocean of life by having a coach. Every orchestra has a music conductor. Every movie has a director. Life is the movie. The coach is the director.

My coaches changed my life. I could not imagine my life without coaches. My father is not only my father but my Godfather. My father was the first coach in my life. My father taught me how to be a man, how to live life for others. My father taught me spirituality. I learned how to pray from my father. My father introduced me to spiritual gurus Lalji Maharaj, HH Pandurang Shastri (DADA), Morari Bapu, Swami Sachidanand. I told my father during my teenage years that I was going to be a priest the world has never seen. My father said to me, "My son, you are the lighthouse for our family." I felt my father's feelings were like emotional blackmail as he wanted me to become a doctor, not a priest. The hunger for spirituality gave me lots of other spiritual gurus in my life like Asharam Bapu, Tejandraprasad, Pramukh Swami, Mahant Swami, Swami Vishwa Anand, Bishop Bira, Pastor Tevon, Dadi Prakashmani, Baba Ramdev, Shivani didi, Sadhvi Rutambhara, Avichal Das & more... I see God, and my Spiritual Guru at the same time. I am going to get blessings from my Guru first. Because of my Guru, I've found God. That's the importance of having a spiritual Guru in life. To become a doctor, you learn from the doctor's professors. To become an engineer, you learn from engineer professors. For an awakening, you need a spiritual Guru. I wish you all the best to find the right spiritual Guru for your awakening. I wrote one full chapter about " My Mentors" in detail in my first "The Celebrity Guru" award-winning book, *You are the Celebrity.*

Click it to get it. (FREE First Chapter)
youarethecelebritybook.com

To become an author, I hired Raymond Aaron as my publisher. Raymond Aaron is the New York Times Bestseller Author of 11+ solo books as well as hundreds and hundreds of coauthored books. Raymond Aaron is the only one in the world to write a book for the *Chicken Soup for the Soul* Book Series as well as a book in the *"Dummies"* book series. Raymond Aaron went to the North Pole in a Polar Race, which is 650 kilometers in a one-month-long foot race to the North Pole. Polar bears were the biggest fear. Raymond Aaron is my Rich Dad as well as a life coach. I learn from Raymond on land, on water, by going on his business cruise retreat, and thousands of miles in the air in business class on a flight. Click it to get it. (FREE Raymond's Book)
RaymondAaron.com
You Gotta Be Hungry.
---Les Brown
You Gotta Be Thirsty.
---#TheCelebrityGuru #DRPPP

To become an international bestseller, I hired Robert J Moore, 5 Times International Bestseller, who wrote about 20 books as well as published many more books.

To become the Guinness World Record holder, I also hired Robert J Moore, Magnetic Entrepreneur Inc.™

Founder. It was my decades-old dream to become the Guinness Book of World Record Holder. God sent me my messenger Robert J Moore to make my dream come true. I wish all the best to Robert J Moore, his beautiful love Faith, as well as Junior Robert, cute Jonathan.

To awaken the author within,
To awaken the coaches within,
To awaken the energy within,
To awaken the spirituality within,
To awaken the Celebrity within,
To awaken the happiness within,

Hire me NOW, yours and the world's only The Celebrity Guru DRPPP.

youarethecelebritybook.com
#4165435231.

Believe in your wildest dreams.
Don't let anybody steal your dreams.
If TRUMP can win, so can you.
You have got a celebrity day.
You have got the celebrity life.
You are the Celebrity.

Dr. Pravin Patel (#DRPPP)

The Celebrity Guru, The Marathon Man, The Himalayas Guru, Humanitarian, Actor, Author, Speaker, Coach, Adventurer.

The Celebrity Guru DR.PPP is the soul that came from the supreme soul and is celebrating life as The Celebrity Guru, The Marathon Man, The Himalayas Guru, The Celebrity Humanitarian, The Celebrity Actor, The Celebrity Author, The Celebrity Speaker, The Celebrity Coach, The Celebrity Adventurer.

The Celebrity Guru DR.PPP's full name is DR Pravin, Prahladbhai Patel. DR. PPP was born on Temple Street, Jhulasan, in the state of Gujarat, India, the home of the family of celebrity NASA astronaut, Sunita Williams, as well as a famous Muslim Goddess Dolo Ma Temple.

The Celebrity Guru DR.PPP has met thousands of celebrities from all over the world, e.g., Bollywood celebrities, Hollywood celebrities, spiritual celebrities, celebrity politicians, celebrity cricketers, celebrity tennis players, celebrity entrepreneurs, celebrity authors, and more. DR.PPP has collected their autographs, photographs, and interviewed them to share their secrets to success with you through his first book, *You are the Celebrity*. It's about how to become famous. To get a free copy of the first chapter of the book, please visit:

youarethecelebritybook.com

DR.PPP studied Medicine in India. DR PPP studied homeopathy in Canada.

DR.PPP served in the Canadian Army as an engineer to fulfill his childhood dream to become an engineer as well as to serve the nation.

For DR. PPP's rates and availability as The Celebrity Speaker as well as The Celebrity Coach, please visit:

youarethecelebritybook.com

Call: 416 543-5231

To awaken the Celebrity within you and 1000000000+ people is his mission, passion, purpose and vision.

The Weekend That Changed my Life
by Stephine Ricker

Ever hear those stories that you thought were fictional? You sit there thinking, "Those stories only happen in the movies, and there is no way that would ever occur to me." You are probably sitting there in your favourite spot on the couch, reading this story. Perhaps, you're thinking of possibilities that are out of your limits, and how would your life change from paying the countless bills that keep coming your way? Maybe you're thinking, "Let's escape in this story as it is possibly better than how my life is and how the current situation is going." Well, yes, read my story, but with a clear understanding that there is a golden road out there, you need to open your mind up for the opportunity to take it!

In April 2019, I saw the brutal end of what seemed like an endlessly long two-year program at Algonquin College. Brutal, more because of the course load which was pressing us students to accomplish the very best that we could become in Baking Management. Students were so profoundly under pressure to achieve, and to be recognized as the star students of the class. The pressure was so great that some students took out their frustration by venting at other students. Also, the course load was intense, for example, Mondays we would have a class starting from 8:00 a.m. to 12:00 p.m., with a half-hour lunch, before our next class at 12:30 p.m. to 7:30 p.m. A lot of nights, I wouldn't be home till 9:00 p.m. and have to return for another 8:00 a.m. class. With the Ottawa winters and our snowstorms, 7:30 a.m., and 8 a.m. classes were the worst to arrive in class on time. Those mornings would begin at 5:00 a.m. Raising children with an overnight-working husband to help me come for the early class wasn't the easiest piece of cake. Here I was, having graduated from college with a two-year diploma, expecting to be hired. My mind was saying, "Finally now, it is over! Possibly now, I will be recognized!"

I passed out my resume mentioning my brand-new diploma, 12 years of kitchen experience and other volunteering experience. Employers give me hits and asked me to come in for interviews. There were no real leads, and my dreams were being shattered. "Why would I go through all the diploma courses, if none of it's going to amount to anything?" I thought.

A month passed; I was sitting on the black leather couch of my mother's living room. My mom was sitting on the sofa in front of me bent over her computer working on her signature program, that she been revamping for six-plus years. My mom states, breaking the silence, "Your sister has done it to me again! Now she refuses to pay her full portion of the rent, which is nine hundred dollars and demands to pay only five hundred dollars for the whole house per month. Plus, she has damaged my property!" My mom owns a four-bedroom house, and my sister wanted the whole house to herself for five hundred dollars per month!

My rent, at this time, for a three-bedroom apartment was one thousand thirty dollars, per month and was considered to be the lowest price in Ottawa. I thought to myself for a moment, "Mom, my husband is currently on summer vacation and off work at the moment, and I am on my college summer break. What if, you and I go down to your house, evict my sister, and get new tenants. I will even spend a month at the house, to occupy it until you can get your next tenants?" I was thinking it would be a way out of the situation, and get the drama at the house to end, so my parents could see a road ahead. My mother and stepfather both looked at each other, talked it over, and in about an hour, we all agreed. My mom and I would be packing up to take a trip to remove my sister the next day.

By this time, I thought to myself her business, would never take off. If it took her this long to create a program, with the amount of cash that she had put towards it. We watched as Holly obtained $100,000 from veteran's affairs, and in less than two months, it was all gone. My husband and I talked about it in hushed voices for years. If Holly couldn't do a functional business with that much money; when we were living paycheck to paycheck, month to month, there was no way we ever could have a functioning business.

So, there I was in the passenger seat of my mother's SUV driving from Ottawa, Ontario, down to London, Ontario. During the trip, we were discussing the plans to remove my sister from the house. We were considering what my sister might try to pull over my mother's head and how that might affect our plans. When I arrived, I had no idea what we were in for. My sister had the only key to the house, so we were forced into a hotel for a week, trying to remove my sister from the damaged property.

"Come see your mom get on stage and receive an award!" stated my mother in this hotel room. This opened an opportunity that changed my life. We drove to Toronto, Ontario, the day before the event was to begin, for my mother to test out the stage. Upon eating lunch at the hotel; this man walks around the corner, wearing jeans and a blue sweatshirt, with short black hair and heavy-set appearance. You could tell by his demeanour that when he enters a room, no matter what he is wearing, the room wants to get to know this man. "Come meet Robert, my coach!" My mother exclaims standing beside him. I arose from my chair, in amazement. "Hello, my name is Stephine Ricker," reaching out to shake his hand. To my surprise, he rejected the handshake and hugged me instead. Instantly, it took me back home to how my father, enters a room and greets people, including myself. I felt so much at home at the moment, that I almost forgot my purse at the table!

We all went downstairs to see the event room together. On the way there, we were introduced to Emilio Roman, International Award-Winning Author of *"101 Ways to Thank a Veteran"*, Speaker and Coach. My mother practiced on stage then asked me, "So how do you think I did?" I responded, "Why are you asking me, when your coach is right behind you?". Robert J. Moore gives the most amazing smile ever and nods in my direction. In that instant, I felt immense pride in my heart. I got the Elite VIP ticket to Magnetic Entrepreneur Author Awards Red Carpet Event 2019. There I was, a nobody, just being given the red carpet treatment along with the stars of the event. Wow! Was I ever excited at that very moment! Robert J. Moore said to me, "I want you there, enjoy this weekend, and soak up everything you can learn from this event!"

We returned the very next day early, at least an hour before the event was supposed to begin. The first day everyone showed up in business attire. I think my mother somehow missed the memo as we were there dressed for the red carpet a day early.

I remember looking for my badge for the Elite VIP pass amongst the others, noticing how one of the Elite VIP tags didn't have a lanyard with it. I wasn't sure who to tell about it, so I mentioned the problem to Robert J. Moore. "I have people who take of that for me," Robert told me. I remember that crystal clear — thinking about how that would feel to be the person who would correct that problem for someone like Robert J. Moore.

It was an inspiring occasion learning everything I could take in with my laptop and cell phone ready to take pictures to download to Facebook. My mother spoke on stage twice that day. Bruce Serbin, Tim Burt and Serena Brown Travis were the judges of the competition that my mother took part in.

Serena Brown Travis is the daughter of renowned motivational speaker Les Brown. Serena strategically intertwines disappointment and defeat with messages of encouragement and inspiration in her children's books. *"Perfect Penny* is assisting me in helping spread positivity into the lives of children and adults. You'll love the tenacity of Perfect Penny. We can all learn from her!" Les Brown states.

For more than 15 years, seven-time US national award-winning publicist and author Bruce Serbin has been a media powerhouse; booking his clients on local and national television and radio shows, in daily local and national newspapers and magazines, and online news outlets.

Bruce is the recipient of seven US national awards, and his work has been recognized by famous organizations.

I learned from Tim Burt, one of the most sought-after International Marketing and Advertising Experts. He'd started out in radio in Rapid City, South Dakota and went on to spend the next 25 years in radio (and other forms of media). The last 16 years, he was employed by CBS Radio, which allowed him to hone his skills in advertising.

Tim's more than 30,000 commercials (Toyota, Burger King, South African Airways, etc.) have generated revenue of over $500 million in global sales.

The second day, when I was preparing for another day of action, who should come over to the table to say 'Hello' but Unstoppable Tracy Schmitt! Standing on the other side of the table, she said: "Hello, what is your business?" The look of shock on my face might have scared her, as I wasn't an entrepreneur at that time, nor did I think I would be. You would have seen the smile light up on Tracy's face, and then I got the opportunity to take pictures of Tracy and my mother.

TV Host Unstoppable Tracy #1 International Mega Success TEDx Speaker. Her mind-blowing story always gets standing ovations pushing audiences out of their limitation zones. In 2019, she has been viewed virally over 30 million views and is the winner of the 2018 #1 Female Transformational Leader out of 160 countries by the John Maxwell Team.

The second day was just as fantastic, and maybe a little more special with the astonishing dresses and awards were given out to the Authors in Magnetic Entrepreneur book series and other published books. The event was so captivating that the magnetic feeling everyone got that day made it hard not to smile and remember it for a lifetime to come.

There was a special lunch for the VIPs and Elite VIPs to eat with the stars of the event. Later, after the meal, when the speaker on stage had finished his high ticket course offer to learn, I sat there in despair, knowing how much I wished I could take his offer, and how my bank account was sitting in the negative. Robert J. Moore approached me directly with the pink slip to the speaker's coaching. I was shocked! Not at all something, I would have figured would happen!

Then, it hit me hard. All this wonderful feeling was going to end, and I would have to go home to a possibly bleak future where I didn't know what would happen. I remember my nana's and stepmom's teachings when I was a young child, "Put on your big girl's panties and go approach the host!" So, I did. I told him that after his event was over, could he explain to me how he went from homeless to successful. I desperately needed a way out for my children and myself, and I needed his guidance. Robert J. Moore said, "Don't you worry, and I can help you!"

A week passed, I helped my mother remove my sister from the house in London, Ontario. During our time in London, Ontario. The employers from the job interviews finally did reach me. I was offered an overnight baker job at Tim Horton's. With a two-year program and twelve years of experience in the kitchen, all it amounted to was to end up in a position that a high school student could have accepted. Personally, it felt like it was a massive slap in the face! So, I rejected the paycheck job.

My mother and I left London, Ontario. On our way home to Ottawa, Robert J. Moore asked us to take a lunch break from the road to meet him for lunch. My mother was astonished when her coaching session with Robert J. Moore became a two-part coaching meeting with me also, and Robert paid for our lunch. "I know how you can become useful." Robert J. Moore began to respond to my question. "Work with your mother for a bit, then come work for me." My eyes became wide with shock. That weekend would amount to one opportunity that wouldn't end! I could hardly believe it! You see, just before the event, Robert J. Moore had fired his event organizer and would need to fill the opening with someone better fitted for the position. I had no idea that I just been interviewed for a career!

Life began to change from that moment on, as Robert J. Moore became true to his word. Serena Brown Travis noticed me amongst the crowd with the daily video blogging I was posting on Facebook. She spoke out my name amongst the masses of International Authors. I got voted into the inner circle from support from Serena Brown Travis, Robert J. Moore and others before I even wrote my first chapter.

I worked for my mother unpaid for over a month. Robert J. Moore decided he liked what I was doing and offered me a contract not only to work for him, but still be coached by him. I still remember that day, and it was one of the happiest moments that my husband and I shared! My husband began to understand that I wasn't just dreaming, that there was a golden road ahead, and it started with what I was doing for Robert J. Moore. The golden way to financial freedom was opening for us, and my husband needs to learn to trust in it.

Robert J. Moore also helped me invest in the best coaches that money could buy to aid me with becoming better fitted for my new career. Bruce Serbin provided me with his high end coaching for public relations. He is teaching me the best way to address media relations to put my clients in the best light for media connections. Tim Burt explained and helped me score my first ad to address the public about my company Ricker's Elite VIP Services. Tracy Lamourie coached me once a week and taught me her media relations program. And, I have had the high honour to remain good friends with Serena Brown Travis.

Ricker's Elite VIP Services, is named after Magnetic Entrepreneur Author Awards 2019, the weekend that changed my life, as Elite VIP was the tag, I was given that weekend.

Tracy Lamourie was a co-host of 89.5FM Toronto CIUT's "Uppercut," and produced weekly news and community segments that aired on television ... of 2011, before her return to Toronto. She's worked at various times as a television host, television producer, and radio host. Tracy and her work on multiple issues have been featured on television broadcasts, e.g. CBC's *The Fifth Estate, Court TV, A & E*, CTV, and more – across North America.

During 2019, I was hired by Robert J. Moore to launch his High-End Mastermind Weekends in September and October and the Magnetic Entrepreneur Author Awards 2020. I learned how to give two-minute and fifteen-minute speeches about my company. I learned the foundations of a reliable business, as well as high impacting courses that people buy for months, even years, of coaching to receive. Robert J. Moore aided me in learning the fast track to success with helping me to become a two-time International Bestselling Author; and Award-winning media relations agency, which has been in magazines and other productions. I have been able to successfully move my family out of poverty, and now we own our own house. We also now own a real estate company and help out other members in our community. All was thanks to Robert J. Moore; we really couldn't have been able to do it successfully without his guidance and support!

So next time the opportunity in your life comes knocking would you take it?

Stephine Ricker

Stephine strives to launch PR promotion events, where she helps the Hosts create their living dream events, and the audience is already booking to attend the next event! Contact Stephine at the sites below:

rickerspromotion@gmail.com
https://www.facebook.com/PR.Event.International/inbox

Conclusion

Thank you for reading this book. Every co-author has worked hard to bring not only their stories but also valuable lessons that you can use to become magnetic yourself.

One of the best ways to become magnetic is to become an author yourself and I would love to help you with that. If you would like to be a part of *The Magnetic Entrepreneur* book series please contact my team at:

> Email - info@magneticentrepreneurinc.com
> Linkedin - www.linkedin.com/in/magneticentrepreneur
> Facebook - Magnetic Entrepreneur Inc.

Become more than you can ever imagine!

Robert J. Moore
Internationally Awarded / Bestselling Author of:
   From Rock Bottom to Success and
     The Better Way Formula – Principles for Success and
       Magnetic Entrepreneur book series
International Speaker

Made in the USA
Lexington, KY
15 December 2019